Hypnosis

How to Harness the Power of Hypnosis to Hypnotize Anyone Now!

Richard Ellsbury

3rd Edition

Table of Contents

Introduction

I want to thank you and congratulate you for purchasing the book, *"Hypnosis: How to Harness the Power of Hypnosis to Hypnotize Anyone Now!"*.

This book contains proven steps and strategies on how to harness the power of hypnosis and to hypnotize anyone directly or indirectly through conversation.

Unbeknownst to most people, hypnosis has plenty of uses in our everyday lives. When done correctly, hypnosis can be used to increase a person's self-esteem, heighten his work productivity, treat his phobias, and help him break away from bad habits. Hypnosis can also help a person lose weight, induce Synesthesia, relieve stress—and a whole lot more!

When the mind is in a state of hypnosis, it becomes open to suggestion. You can embed an idea, an image, and even a memory into the human mind. By simply planting a suggestion into the subconscious, you are able to influence a person's behavior in real life.

By unveiling the secrets of covert hypnotism, one can become a brilliant conversationalist. You can even perform hypnosis on yourself to increase motivation and to ensure success in your career and in your personal life.

Thanks again for purchasing this book, I hope you enjoy it!

Chapter 1

Understanding Hypnosis

Most people's views about hypnosis are guided by what they see in movies. So when you hear the word, you may immediately think of a goateed man, wearing a big hat, holding a staff on one hand and waving a pocket watch on the other. Back and forth, he swings it until his subject reaches a zombie-like state, robbed off of his free will and under the evil spell of the goateed hypnotist.

The unfortunate hypnotized victim will then be compelled to obey the hypnotist's command, no questions asked, but real life isn't like in the movies as you know. Actual hypnosis has little or zero resemblance to how it is portrayed in movies, TV and comic books. They are called works of fiction for a reason.

Hypnosis is one of the most mysterious and understandably misunderstood concepts. As a matter of fact, it has been the subject of debate for over 200 years. What a lot of people do not know is that people have been entering a trance for thousands of years. This hypnotic trance is induced in various forms of meditation, which many cultures practice. Nobody seemed to notice it until in the late 1700s.

The first scientific conception of hypnotism came from an Austrian physician, Franz Mesner, who is now recognized as the father of modern hypnotism. Back in those times though, his concept of hypnotism was not recognized.

Mesmer defined hypnosis as a mystical force that flows from the hypnotist to the subject. He called this event animal magnetism. Critics were thrown off by the mere mention of magic in his definition. However, his assumption of the power coming from a hypnotist and applied to a subject stuck for quite some time.

So what really is hypnosis?

Hypnosis hails from the Greek word *hypnos*, meaning sleep. However, hypnosis is not a state of sleep. In fact, during hypnosis, an individual is in a conscious state. He possesses heightened focus and concentration. His imagination is intensified as well. Every other stimulus around him is blotted out. By reducing peripheral awareness, he is able to focus his attention on a specific thought or a memory and his capacity to respond to suggestion is increased.

With this said, real life hypnosis contradicts the popular yet misguided conception of hypnosis in the movies. First off, when a person is hypnotized, he is not in a semi-sleep state. He is actually awake, aware and hyper-attentive, which also brings us to the second point of contradiction. A person who is in a hypnotic trance does not lose his free will. He does not become a slave to the hypnotist.

Unbeknownst to most people, they frequently experience being in this state of human consciousness. In truth, people subject themselves to self-hypnosis every day. Have you ever lost yourself in a really good book? Have you ever been so engrossed in your current activity that you're momentarily able to forget about the time or your surroundings? During all of these activities, people are not exactly asleep. They are alert the entire time. However, their attention is so concentrated to the point that almost every other thought has been excluded.

When a person is in a trance state, he is relaxed. The mind is more uninhibited. The individual is less conscious about his behavior. Notice that whenever you go to the movies you are able to temporarily forget about your problems at work or at home. Whenever people watch a film, they tend to experience feelings of happiness whenever a pleasant scene or a happy ending is revealed. Their hearts beat faster when the monster in a horror flick jumps out of nowhere. This, in itself, is a form of hypnotism.

How Hypnotism Works

There are plenty of theories built around hypnosis but this is the predominant one. Hypnosis is perceived as a way of accessing someone's subconscious mind directly.

Our subconscious mind works hand in hand in with our conscious mind. While the latter makes us aware of facts, the former is in the backseat, giving us access to memory. Our conscious mind makes us think critically and realistically and our subconscious makes us think more freely with imagination and impulse.

When we are trying to solve a problem for instance, we assess the facts and brainstorm ideas for solutions consciously, but more often than not, the "aha" moments come to us unconsciously. It's like being stuck on a problem then thinking about a solution out of the blue. The thought comes from our subconscious.

The subconscious is also responsible for the things that we do automatically like breathing. It is also the one that processes and interprets the physical information that we receive through our bodies. In other words, the conscious mind may be at the forefront, but it is our subconscious that works behind the operation. The key to getting access to the subconscious directly without being filtered by the conscious mind is hypnosis.

According to psychiatrists, focusing and deep relaxation techniques are effective in making us feel calm. They also work in subduing our consciousness so it moves to the backseat while the subconscious is brought to the forefront. This is why during the process of hypnosis a person still has complete awareness but is highly suggestible.

Keep in mind that the unconscious mind seeks freedom while

the conscious mind seeks to filter. What the hypnotist does is to speak directly to the subject's subconscious. With the conscious mind placed in the backseat, the more imaginative and impulsive subconscious is in control. The person's reactions to suggestions and compulsions are more automatic. Because it is the subconscious that controls the body's senses—visual, tactile, auditory, etc.—as well the emotions, the hypnotist is able to trigger the subject's feelings. More than that, it is in the subconscious where a person's memory is stored. Therefore, during hypnosis, the individual is able to access events in the past that have long been buried away. By digging up these memories, psychiatrists are able to help a client resolve his present issues. Furthermore, since the mind is in a suggestible state during hypnosis, it is possible to fabricate false memories. For this reason, psychiatrists must take special care when using hypnosis to access a patient's memory of the past.

Fallacies involving Hypnosis

Thanks to popular Hollywood fiction, several misconceptions have been formed about hypnosis. Before you are able to harness the power of hypnotism, you must first understand what it is and what it is not.

- One common fallacy involving hypnotism is that it will enable you to take control of the person's mind. On the contrary, only you can control your own mind. The job of the hypnotist is to provide the subject with the suggestions. The subject's subconscious will either agree or disagree with that suggestion. If an idea is strongly unappealing to an individual, his subconscious will automatically reject it.

- If you believe that you can use hypnotism to instantly make a person roll over like a dog, then think again. While it is true that the person is momentarily stripped of some common inhibitions while in a state of trance, hypnotism requires trust in order to be successful. In order for any hypnosis technique to work, the subject must be able to feel safe. More than that, during hypnosis, a person's sense of safety and morality remains intact. Simply put, you can't just ask someone to do whatever it is that you want them to do.

- Another common misconception brought about by its frequent use in fictional works is that hypnosis is evil or supernatural. The fact is hypnosis is a natural human state. More than that, hypnotherapy has been studied scientifically by the most prominent psychologists of their time such as Dr. Sigmund Freud, Dr. Carl Jung, and Dr. Erikson Milton.

- Contrary to what you may have seen in the movies, there is no danger of a person remaining in a "zombie-like" trance after hypnotism. During hypnosis, a person is in a state of hyper-awareness. In the presence of a danger, he will easily be able to emerge from the hypnotic state.

- While it is true that it can be used to create permanent improvements in a person, from treating phobias to increasing self-esteem, hypnosis is not an instant cure for all of your problems. With hypnotherapy and certain lifestyle changes, each person will be able to create progress at his own pace and in his own time.

- One cannot rely on hypnosis to get the subject to confess to something. It is for this reason that hypnotism is not an accepted alternative for lie detector tests.

- Also, some people believe that after undergoing hypnosis, a person will not be able to remember anything. As mentioned, the subject is not asleep during hypnosis. He, in fact, has an increased sense of awareness. Even his sense of hearing is heightened during a hypnotism session.

- Another popular myth is that there are people who are immune to hypnotism. As said before, we have all been in a state of hypnosis and it continues to happen every day. Before we fall asleep at night and before we are fully awake in the morning, we are in a state of hypnosis. More than that, the fact that you are reading this book means that you have already opened your mind to the very idea of hypnotism.

Traditional Hypnosis vs. Covert Hypnosis

In conventional hypnosis, the hypnotist provides suggestions to the subject and the subject approaches it as if it were reality. For example, if the hypnotist suggests to the subject that his arm has gone numb, the person will then act as though he cannot move or feel his own arm. If the hypnotist suggests to the subject that he is in a very hot room, then the subject will begin to feel the warmth and he will begin to sweat. However, during the entire session, the subject is aware that it is all unreal.

The same thing happens when you read a good book or watch a suspense film. You become so into what is going on, you feel the emotions the characters may be feeling. You forget everything else because you are so focused on a scene. At the same time, you are aware of reality and you are well capable of distinguishing fantasy from what you are reading or watching and your own reality.

During a state of hypnosis, you become relaxed and uninhibited. At this state, you are also more open to suggestions. Conventional hypnotists guides you to reach this state so a goal whether to quit a bad habit or enforce a more positive one can be achieved. As the hypnotist offers suggestions, you tend to embrace them.

A lot of people are hesitant about the idea of being hypnotized because they are afraid that they may make a fool of themselves. The truth is a hypnotist cannot make you do anything that violates your morality and sense of safety. You have your free will. You still are your own person. Unless you really want to cluck like a chicken, a hypnotist won't be able to make you.

Today, traditional hypnosis is becoming more popular and accepted by the public. Hypnotists offer their services to people facing serious issues about their health and personal lives. People who find it difficult to quit smoking for instance, can walk in a session to help them correct their bad habits. In this sense, the client or subject is aware and willingly participates in the session. The hypnotist will explain what will be done and what to expect. In other words, it is a straightforward process.

Covert hypnosis, on the other hand, is done without the subject's knowledge. The hypnotist influences the subject's emotions through conversation. The hypnotist may use some tactics and keywords to make a person more suggestible. It's like being forced to sit through a movie you really don't want to see. You're hesitant at first but it may also grow on you. Just like with traditional hypnosis, however, a hypnotist using a covert method cannot force someone to do anything stupid or immoral unless the person is willing to do it.

With all these said, hypnosis is really still a mystery. It has a lot to do with how the brain works. It's marvelous but it is NOT supernatural.

Chapter 2

What Else Do You Need to Know about Hypnosis?

After the brief introduction to hypnosis, you probably still have a lot of questions left. We will cover as much of these questions as we can in this chapter.

The methods used by hypnotists vary. Whatever method is used, the following basic prerequisites must be followed. One, the person must want to go through hypnosis. Two, the person must believe in the process and that he can be hypnotized. Three, the person must be made relaxed and comfortable. When these things are fulfilled, the hypnotist can start guiding the subject to a trance. While methods vary from one hypnotist to another, the most commonly used ones are the following.

Eye Fixation or Fixed Gaze Induction

This is the method we are all familiar with. Remember the mysterious goateed man in the movies, TV and comics? This is what he uses. He waves a pocket watch to put his subject into a hypnotic trance.

The idea of this method is that by encouraging the subject to focus intently on a single object, he can be able to disregard other stimuli. As he focuses, the hypnotist will talk to him in a low tone of voice. This will make the subject feel relaxed so he can become suggestible.

Eye Fixation has been widely used in the past especially in the early years of hypnosis. It is no longer as popular today simply because it can neither work nor be used on a large number of people.

The main intention of this method is to help the subject become highly focused to the point of being stimulated to sleep. While swinging a pocket watch is a technique popularized by works of fiction, it is hardly the only way to apply the method. If you want to use the eye fixation method to hypnotize someone, you can ask the subject to raise his eyes upward and focus on a specific spot on the ceiling.

You can then start to suggest in a low tone that the muscles in his eyelids are getting tired and heavier at each passing time. You can then suggest to your subject to allow their eyelids to close. When your subject rolls his eyes upward and closes his eyelids, he sends a signal to his subconscious that it's time to sleep. At this point, the subject is much more open to suggestions.

Rapid

While the previous technique works by lulling a subject to a hypnotic trance, this one works just as well by overloading a subject's mind with firm and sudden commands. For this technique to work, the hypnotist must give forceful commands. The authoritative tone must be convincing enough to make the subject surrender to the situation and give up his conscious control.

Stage hypnotists are usually the ones who use this technique. They take advantage of the subject's feeling on edge as he is presented before an audience. The situation itself makes a subject susceptible to hypnotism.

Progressive Relaxation

If stage hypnotists have the rapid technique, psychiatrists rely on the progressive relaxation technique. It uses a completely opposite strategy than the previous technique. Rather than employing sudden and forceful commands, the progressive relaxation technique uses a soothingly slow tone of voice. Through this, the hypnotist makes the subject feel completely focused and relaxed. This is a technique commonly used in self-hypnosis training and in meditation and relaxation audio tapes.

The method is called progressive relaxation because it focuses on relaxing one body area at a time. Here's a sample sequence.

- Feel a calming energy landing on your scalp at the top of your head and sliding to your nape.
- Feel the ball of energy relaxing your forehead.
- Now, relax your eyes.

- Feel the calming energy moving down to your cheekbones.
- Feel the muscles on your jaw and mouth relax.
- The ball of energy is now moving to your neck and shoulders. You feel these parts of your body slowly relax.
- You now feel the energy easing down to your upper arms, elbows, forearms, hands and fingers. You feel every bit of you relax.
- A warm energy now fills your back and chest.
- The warmth extends to your abdomen giving you a feeling of ultimate relaxation.
- You feel your pelvis and hip area soften.
- You thigh muscles now feel much more relaxed.
- The warmth settles on your knees.
- The calming energy eases down to your calf. You feel every bit of muscles relax.
- You can feel warmth passing from your feet to your toes. You now feel warm and absolutely relaxed.

Guided Imagery

This method works not only in inducing a subject into a hypnotic state, but also in deepening it. By using imagery suggestions, the subject is guided to a journey of relaxation. It also helps the mind become highly focused.

There are various ways of using this method. It can also be employed for self-hypnosis. Among the most common examples include a journey to the beach, forest, long hallways and climbing down a staircase. It works effectively because the human mind, specifically, the subconscious responds well to imagery and symbols.

We've mentioned earlier about the three criteria that must be fulfilled before inducing a subject to a full trance. Hypnotists usually use a test in order to assess a subject's capacity and willingness to undergo hypnosis. Among the most common tests include making simple suggestions like "Relax your arms." The hypnotist will then work way up to making more complex suggestions like asking the subject to distort normal thoughts or suspend disbelief. A typical example script is, "Pretend you as weightless as a feather floating through the air."

So how long will it take for a subject to enter a hypnotic state?

There is no standard number of minutes that applies to everyone. The amount of time needed to put a person under a state of hypnosis varies. It depends on the person's personality and mental state. With this said, some people may only need a few minutes while others may require over 30 minutes.

The amount of time required for a person to enter a state of hypnosis also varies depending on the situation. For instance, a woman in labor who prefers using hypnosis for pain relief over general anesthetic during childbirth may require a deeper level of trance.

How does it feel like to be hypnotized?

The experience is not the same for everyone. It varies dramatically from one subject to another. There are some who report a feeling of extreme relaxation and others feel a sense of detachment. Still, there are other hypnotized subjects who say they feel like what they do during hypnosis is outside their consciousness.

Ernest Hilgard, a researcher on hypnosis, performed an experiment demonstrating how much hypnosis can significantly alter a subject's perception. He instructed a subject to feel no pain in his arm, which was then put in iced water. An individual who was not hypnotized will remove his arm from the iced water after only a few seconds because naturally, he feels pain in his arm. On the other hand, hypnotized subjects were able to keep their arms there for a couple of minutes and not feel pain.

What purpose does hypnosis serves?

Several research studies have been and continue to be conducted about the applications of hypnosis. So far, the following benefits have been proven.

- Hypnosis can help treat chronic pain like with patients suffering from rheumatoid arthritis.
- Hypnosis is useful in treating or reducing a woman's pain during childbirth.
- Hypnosis has also proven effective in alleviating the symptoms of dementia.
- Hypnotherapy is also helpful in treating certain ADHD symptoms.
- Hypnosis may also help in relieving cancer patients from the side effects of chemotherapy including vomiting and nausea.
- It may also be used in reducing pain experienced in dental procedures.
- It may also be beneficial in individuals suffering from skin conditions such as psoriasis and warts.
- Individuals suffering from the symptoms of Irritable Bowel Syndrome may also find hypnotherapy quite useful.

However, the benefits of hypnosis are not limited to these. Hypnotherapy is also used in helping individuals cope with certain problems like anxiety, phobia, weight and bad habits like smoking and gambling.

How do I know if I or another person can be hypnotized?

A lot of people think hypnosis is not possible and feel that they are immune. Research results however, contradict this belief. According to studies, a large portion of the population can be hypnotized, even people who think they are not hypnotizable.

There are approximately 10 percent of adults who are considered either impossible or difficult to hypnotize. However, 15 percent of the population is very much responsive to hypnotic suggestions. As compared to adults, children are more prone to hypnosis. Among the people who can be hypnotized, those who are easily absorbed in fantasies prove to be the most responsive.

Because of their imaginative nature, children are naturally more responsive to hypnosis. Today, hypnotherapy is used in children for treating anxiety, confidence issues, medical conditions and behavioral problems. For the therapy to work however, it is important that the person treating a child subject must be well versed in the particular issue the child is suffering from.

Individuals who find it easier to relax are generally more responsive to hypnosis. Others can only experience a light trance while others can go deeper. For the purpose of hypnotherapy though, a light trance is sufficient for enabling a patient to reap the benefits of the therapy.

Hypnosis requires an open mind. Research cannot agree more. In order to reap positive results, a subject must have a positive view of the process. If you want to use hypnosis to improve your lifestyle and general well-being, you must keep an open mind.

How is it possible for a treatment of the mind to affect the body?

The human body is physically responsive to thoughts. This is why when we watch a gruesome movie with a character being wounded, we somehow relate to the physical pain. If we think of thoughts that make us fearful, we start seating and shaking. In the same way, when we think about calming thoughts, our muscles start to relax. We breathe more deeply and our heart rates stabilize.

Scientists call them autonomic nervous system responses. They are involuntary and are useful promoting health and well-being. For this reason, psychiatrists and hypnotherapists use hypnosis to help out patients in diminishing negative physical reactions and replacing them with positive ones.

Will hypnosis put me to sleep? Will I be unconscious during the trance?

This misunderstanding about hypnosis emanates from what is suggested by its Greek root word, “hypnos” meaning sleep. The truth is hypnosis is not equivalent to sleep. A hypnotized person is not asleep. Rather, he is in a relaxed state with heightened awareness.

This comes as a surprise to many people who undergo hypnosis. They think that the session did not work because they were conscious all the time during the session and this is exactly the point of hypnosis. It is not meant for a hypnotist or a psychiatrist to take over a person's mind. A hypnotized person is capable of answering questions and asking them. It is not a mysterious experience for the subject but its results can be very substantial.

Will a hypnotized person lose control of himself?

This relates back to the previous answer. Because a person under a hypnotic trance is not asleep or unconscious, it is not possible for a subject to lose control of himself. The main goal of hypnosis is to make a person feel more relaxed, hesitant and less distracted so that his subconscious mind comes through.

Our conscious mind is indeed essential. However, it does serve as barrier for us to use our mental abilities in a more constructive way. By putting our subconscious in the front seat, we can achieve more, even the things that we don't think (with our conscious minds) are possible.

So during a hypnotic state, a subject won't say or do anything he does not want subconsciously. A hypnotized person is still in control and can act in his own will.

Is it possible to be trapped in a hypnotic trance?

No. Anyone who is hypnotized can come back from it. Coming out of a trance is not the problem. For some people, getting in a trance is the issue, so no one can be hypnotized indefinitely.

If I am hypnotized, can I remember past events more accurately?

No, it is not a guarantee. Although being in a hypnotic trance may help a person re-experience past events, there is no guarantee that he will remember them correctly. What a hypnotist can do is only to help the subject recall perceptions.

This misconception is probably in reference to crime drama and movies where witnesses are hypnotized into remembering accurate details about an event. In reality however, it does not happen. Hypnosis cannot be used to uncover truths, only perceptions.

I hope I have covered most of your basic concerns about hypnosis. Moving forward, we will go through specific hypnosis methods and how we can apply them in an effective manner.

Chapter 3

Direct Suggestion Hypnosis

This method can be used successfully as long as its use is in accordance to the issues the client is dealing with. For a direct suggestion to work, it must be used to touch on the subject's core belief system. Every suggestion must be specific to the subject. This will make him a lot more responsive and accepting.

It is also important for direct suggestions to be delivered authoritatively. However, the suggestions may also be delivered gently like in a casual conversation. Still, direct suggestions may be inserted in a story or metaphors. No matter how the suggestions are delivered, they should follow the most important rule. That is the suggestions must be completely relevant to the subject, targeting his core belief system directly.

Direct suggestion hypnosis technique works by planting concepts directly into the person's mind. The world is represented in a human being's mind by images. Which is why whenever he hears a word, he must first access memories related to that word before he is able to understand that word. The effectiveness of direct suggestion lies in the fact that it may be used to target a person's specific issues. This means that in order for it to be effective, the hypnotist must first know some facts about the subject. When the hypnotist is able to hit the correct spot, it increases the chance that the suggestion will be accepted by the individual.

The mind works in such a way that what the person visualizes, he obtains. The suggestions provided in hypnosis create powerful images for the individual. When health or anything positive is suggested during hypnosis the subconscious works in order to turn it into reality.

Using Direct Suggestions

- **Repetition**

The more a direct suggestion is repeated to the person, the more effective it becomes. However, be careful about repeating the same words. The key is in finding many different ways on how to present the same idea. It may be repeated in various parts of the session.

Correct: "You like your job. Your job provides you with a sense of satisfaction. Your work brings out the best in you. Your occupation provides you with a sense of purpose. You enjoy learning new things while you work. Your job enables you to grow as a person."

Wrong: "From now on, you will love your job."

Notice that in the sample script, the same thought is conversed in different ways. It also provides reasons for loving a job. It targets specific core beliefs like the need for personal growth, satisfaction, sense of purpose and direction, etc.

- **Positive Wording**

An important thing to remember when using direct suggestion is that your words must conjure images of things that the subject wants. If you're not careful with your words, you might end up invoking the opposite.

Correct: "You enjoy being with people and talking with them. You are confident whenever you are in a crowd."

Wrong: "You are no longer afraid of people. You no longer feel nervous when you are speaking in front of a huge crowd. You no longer worry that they will judge you. You're no longer afraid that they will see through you and think you are a fraud. "

Psychiatrists use positive phrasing for a reason. Negative words paint a negative picture. For instance, if you tell someone that he should not be afraid of people, the mere mention of fear makes that person nervous. You can tell the person to not think about being judged, but he will only feel overwhelmed with images of people judging him. In other words, you (although unintentionally) help enforce the same things that you want that person to forget about by using negative wording. This is why it is important to create positive imagery using positive statements like the first example does.

- **Take it to the Present**

When using direct suggestion, be sure to deliver the idea in the present tense. Suggest to the subconscious that it is now part of the person's present life and not something that is in the distant future. When you give the suggestion in the future tense, you're risking the chance that it may never occur.

Correct: "You are able to sleep well at night."

Wrong: "You will be able to sleep well soon."

This is another important thing. The suggestion can become more real to the person if you make him feel like it is happening now. You eliminate a chance of it not coming true because it is already happening as you speak.

- **Reflection**

The direct suggestion should be able to reflect the subject's experience.

Correct: "You exhibit confidence in everything that you do, from greeting a stranger to parking your car."

Wrong: "You exhibit confidence as you perform in front of everyone. (This is not relevant unless the person plays an instrument, or acts, or sings, etc. in public)

When using the direct suggestion method, it is important to know something about the person. You can craft direct suggestions according to his personal experiences. Although the second example is phrased beautifully, it is not relevant to everyone and it may not be to your subject. You have to be specific to the subject's experiences so it will help to get to know them first.

Do you ever wonder why it's much easier to convince a friend rather than a stranger? It's because you know your friend. You know how to get through to them because you are familiar with their experiences. You can make effective suggestions by being familiar with the subject's life.

- **The Subject's Beliefs**

To increase its effectiveness, it is necessary to base the suggestion on the person's beliefs. For instance, if the subject believes in karma, then tell him that success in life is their positive karma. Use metaphors so that the person will be able to relate to what you are suggesting.

Correct: "The universe's reward for you is success. You are on your way there. As of this moment, confidence is building within you. You are ready to change. You are willing to change. You are ready to take what is yours."

Wrong: "There is no such thing as karma. You achieve success when you go after it and grab it."

Beliefs are important to everyone. Getting to know your subject's core belief system is not only important in crafting effective direct suggestions. It is also essential in avoiding direct suggestions that may contradict his belief system. The moment you deliver a suggestion that goes against his core beliefs, you run the risk of losing his responsiveness to your words.

- **Focus**

Effective direct suggestion requires dealing with one issue at a time. For example, a person is suffering from both gambling addiction and insomnia. It is best to address these problems in two separate sessions because each suggestion in each session must be meant to support each other.

Correct: "You are able to sleep well at night. While sleeping, your body is able to recharge itself so that when you wake up in the morning, you feel happy and energized."

Wrong: "You are able to sleep well at night and you are able to resist gambling. You no longer feel the urge to smoke."

The fact is it is quite impossible to address all issues at once. Do not rush the process. If you want to be as effective as possible, you have to focus on one specific issue at a time.

- **Be Thorough**

As much as possible, it is necessary to address every possible aspect of the issue. Instead of suggesting a complete solution, there should be a series of suggestions that support each other and eventually leads towards a solution.

Correct: "You speak with confidence. Your voice is steady and firm. You look at people directly in the eyes when you talk to them. You are able to communicate your feelings. You walk with confidence. You are aware that each stride has a purpose. With the confident way in which you move, you are showing the world that you are a worthwhile person."

Wrong: "You are always confident when you're around people."

Remember to cover all your bases. Do not leave any stone unturned. Ask yourself what are the issues this person is facing. What kind of situations had he been through in relation to each issue? Make sure you include them in your suggestions. In other words, you must go through each issue thoroughly.

- **The Subject's Experience**

Use the person's experiences so that he will be able to relate more with the suggestion. For example, if he mentioned that he had won an amateur poetry contest, then take advantage of that information in delivering your suggestion.

Correct: "You are able to feel the confidence building inside you. It's that very same feeling that you have felt when you won that poetry competition. That time when you were able to show everyone how well you write and how skilled you are in communicating your feelings..."

Wrong: "You must have achieved something in the past that you are proud of. Gain confidence from that moment."

Use the subject's experiences, both negative and positive, to reinforce the suggestions. Help your subject celebrate his successes. It is a huge confidence booster that contributes to motivation so he can achieve what he wants to whether it is losing weight, overcoming social phobia or quitting smoking.

- **Emphasizing the Subject's Assets**

Often, individuals are unaware of what they have. They tend to overlook and belittle their resources. Use the person's background in order to identify possible areas of strength. For example, the subject has revealed to you a particular job crisis which he had to solve by himself. Through mentioning this, you are able to remind him of his capabilities.

Correct: "Remember that time when you had that incident at work. You were able to deal with the problem singlehandedly. This shows that you have an ability to think straight and to prioritize during crisis situations."

Wrong: "Try searching for any resources from within you. Perhaps you know of a personal strength..."

- **Be Realistic**

Any suggestions made must be achievable by the individual. They must be positive and they must stretch the person's possibilities but they must also be realistic and in line with a person's capability. Remember that the subject may be able to reject a suggestion if he wishes to and any suggestion that seems unattainable will automatically be rejected by his subconscious.

Correct: "You respect your body. You are able to control what you eat. You can prepare healthy, well-balanced meals and enjoy eating them in moderation. You are on your way towards experiencing its gradual positive effects on your body."

Wrong: "You will lose weight within this week. You will start looking attractive and everyone will begin to notice you and your transformation."

- **Avoid Suggestions Set up for Failure**

Some hypnotists make the mistake of being careless with their words. Avoid using absolutes like "never", "always", and "all the time". Otherwise, your suggestion is meant to fail from the very beginning. Be sure to match the suggestion according to each individual's lifestyle and capability.

Correct: "You can find time in dedicating yourself towards your goal. You can use the tiny spurts of energy in between chores to work on your goal."

Wrong: "You will work on your goal every day. You will dedicate all of your time towards achieving your goal." (A busy person's subconscious is likely to automatically reject this suggestion.)

- **Engage the Senses**

Keep in mind that each individual is able to experience the world in his own unique way. To form a big impact, you must be sure to engage all of the person's senses during hypnosis. For instance, limiting yourself to visual metaphors is unlikely to work on a subject who is unable to visualize very well.

Correct: "Imagine yourself in that party. You see the people looking at you. They notice your confidence. They see your smile and they smile back. You hear them greeting you. You hear the soft music playing in the background and you know that you're going to have a good time."

- **Focus on the Subject's Behavior**

You should always bear in mind that the suggestions are meant only to influence the individual's behavior. Making suggestions that involve the behavior of other people is misleading and is likely to result to disappointment.

Correct: "Every day, you do something to prove to your children that you deserve their respect. You earn their respect by providing for them. You communicate openly with your children. You show them that they have your support."

Wrong: "Your children have accepted you for what you are. They love you and they respect you."

- **Use Strong Emotions**

Suggestions work better when the behaviors are related to powerful emotions.

Correct: "When you open your eyes, with each second, your concentration increases. Your mind grows more focused. Your vision is sharp. Your body feels alive. There's something stirring from within you. It's a feeling of anticipation for the new day. The new 'you' is ready to face the new day."

Wrong: "When you wake up, you will feel recharged."

- **Support Suggestion with Logic**

Subjects are able to receive suggestions better if they are supported by reason. However, keep in mind that the mind under hypnosis does not have the ability for full critical thinking so what's needed here is implied hypnotic logic.

Correct: "You have spent enough time observing other people's lives. Now it's time to work on yours. And when you think of all the successes of those other people that you know, think of how you deserve the same thing. And think of how you are able to achieve that success when you stop drinking. You can stop drinking today."

Wrong: "You can stop drinking today."

- **Simplicity is the Key**

Speaking to the mind in its subconscious state is like talking to the mind of a child. Make sure that you choose words that are simple, short, and direct and those that create the most impact. If you use long and complex sentences, your words are likely to be ignored.

Correct: “You want to be happy. You want to make your family happy. You want to save money. You are ready to let go of your gambling habits.”

Wrong: “Habitual gambling can cause serious detrimental effects to an individual’s personal and social life. You will see a marked increase in your finances and an improvement in your social relationships if you decide to abstain from gambling.”

Chapter 4

Conversational Hypnosis

Conversational hypnosis utilizes indirect suggestion. The words are intended to mislead and confuse the subject about its meaning, the possibilities of the suggestion, and the suggestion's relationship with the person. By using The Milton Model, hypnosis can be done under the guise of normal everyday conversation. Because the hypnotic words are indirect and hence, not easily defined, the subject actually pauses and searches their subconscious mind in order to understand what the words mean and how they apply to them personally. This is called the transderivational search. When the individual does this, he will actually find something in his memory that will fit with those words.

The Milton Model can be more effective than direct suggestion because it yields less resistance. For instance, people who suffer from extremely low self-esteem may have a hard time accepting direct suggestions such as "You deserve to be successful." However, they will become more open to indirect suggestions like "I wonder how aware you are that you have the ability to achieve success... and that you have several qualities, many qualities that can make a person successful."

Suggestions for Conversational Hypnosis

- **Cause-Effect Implied and Complex Equivalence**

What the hypnotist does is to make a statement and then implies that there is a direct relationship between that statement and the next statement. For example you may state a true statement and then make another statement which is false. However, you will trick the subject into believing that since the first statement is true, therefore, the next statement is also true.

"You know that you can stop smoking. This <u>means</u> that you have the right to stop."

"Seeing yourself climb those stairs <u>means</u> that you have decided to pursue your higher goals."

- **Truism Sets**

This is done by stating the obvious to yield a false cause and effect.

"Everyone likes to succeed. Everyone deserves to succeed. You deserve to succeed."

While a stubborn conscious mind may say yes to both the first and the second statements, it may doubt the third statement. The unconscious mind however, can be tricked into agreeing with statement 3 simply because statements 1 and 2 are true.

➢ Conversational Postulate

This refers to those questions which may seem as though you are asking for a Yes or No answer but you are really manipulating the person to perform a particular behavior. These are, in fact, instructions disguised as questions.

"I wonder if you could imagine that you are standing in the middle of a bridge...?"

➢ Embedded Commands

This is when you insert commands in what may seem like usual conversation. This is used with analogical marking. For instance, the hypnotist may raise his voice or alter the tone of his voice while embedding the command.

"I can see how RELAXED you are lying on that chair... So PEACEFUL... so CONFIDENT... It looks as though you are ready to LET THINGS GO as I talk about things. It looks like you know that you can just RELAX and FLOAT AWAY towards somewhere nice... RELAXING... as you slow DOWN... going DEEPER... and DEEPER..."

➢ Presuppositions

This is done by beginning with an assumption that the statement is true and then immediately jumping off into the consequence of that statement being true. This is to avoid bringing up the core concept of that statement, thus, allowing the subconscious to pass it off as a fact instead of testing whether it is true or false.

"Because you are now more relaxed, you will begin to feel something else..."

In this suggestion, the subject doesn't question whether he is really more relaxed. His subconscious is already forced to accept it as a fact. The mind is too busy digesting the idea of the consequence that it doesn't have time to challenge the previous statement.

- **Extended Quotation**

This is done by attributing one's words to another person so that the suggestion will meet less resistance from the subject.

"There was once a teacher who said that 'Change really begins from within' and that 'Anyone can change if they really want to.'"

- **Lost Performative**

This is when a suggestion is provided to a person as a fact but is not supported by proof. The intention of the hypnotist is to let the subconscious accept it as a self-evident fact.

"The answer lies somewhere within your subconscious mind."

- **Tag Question**

These are questions designed to urge the subject to agree with the statement. When asking tag questions, be sure to use a descending tone because this lessens the likelihood of disapproval.

"This chair is very relaxing, isn't it?"

- **Mind Reading**

Although the hypnotist has no idea what the subject may be thinking or feeling, the suggestion gives off that impression.

"Your mind is now wondering about how all this will turn into a reality..."

- **Modal Operator**

This is the use of words to imply the possibility of something happening. The Milton Model typically uses words like will, would, can, could, should, etc.

"And each exhalation will bring about more relaxation..."

- **Inanimations**

This is done by assigning emotions to objects and thoughts that cannot possibly have feelings. The subconscious mind is open to metaphors and will therefore, be able to accept this suggestion.

"The part of you that causes you to gamble is ashamed of what it's done to your life. That part of you wants to change for the better."

- **Negative Suggestions**

The unconscious mind tends to omit negative words like

"don't". When you say "Don't imagine a red balloon", it is more likely to make the subject conjure up an image of a red balloon. Negative suggestions work by saying one thing to create a different effect.

"I don't want you to feel like you are going too deep... deeper and deeper into trance."

- **Unspecific Objects and Verbs**

This is when you use vague words which the subconscious mind tends to accept in context. What happens here is that the subconscious creates its own meaning for the vague words. It searches its memory for something to connect the word with.

"And you will gather all of the resources from within you..."

The conscious mind may ask "What resources?" but the unconscious mind, instead of asking, automatically looks within for what can be connected to these resources. Politicians often use this trick.

Chapter 5

Basic Hypnosis

The first step for performing basic hypnosis is to select a comfortable environment. The location need not be completely quiet but it should be free from sudden noises that may interrupt the activity. As you speak to the subject, be sure to do it in a calm and slow manner. Observe pauses with each key statement. In the following script, it is necessary to note that the ellipses mean you should pause after the word. Also, you may choose not to follow the script by word. This only serves as a guide so you may change the words as the situation demands.

- Tell the subject to relax his muscles.

It is important to get rid of the subject's anxieties and to relieve the tension in his muscles.

You: *Settle down... You are beginning to relax...Shrug your shoulders and release the tension... Your shoulders are loose and limp... You will lift your arms a little and then drop them...*

- Ask the subject to rotate his head. Instruct him to gradually remove the tension from the neck, then down to the back, and finally to the legs.

- Next, instruct the subject to focus on his breathing. This helps to slow it down.

You: *Take a deep breath... Exhale... Now, inhale deeply... Let it out... Allow yourself to relax more as you exhale... Now, inhale once more... and as you let go, allow yourself to relax fully...*

Then provide the subject with your approval by saying something affirming.

You: *Good...*

- The next step would be to direct the person's attention towards something. The purpose of this is to eliminate any thoughts that might distract him.

You: *You are now aware of your breathing... you are aware of the movement of your breath...*

Tell the subject that with each time that he exhales, he is able to relax more and more. Remind him constantly of how he is feeling more relaxed with each out-breath. Tell him that as he is starting to feel tired. By doing this, you are now pacing and leading the person's behavior.

- Instruct the subject to close his eyelids. The more you suggest to him that he is feeling tired and heavy, the more his chances of obeying you increases.

You: *Be aware that the deeper and deeper you go... you become more and more comfortable...*

Suggest to the subject that he is aware of how nice it feels to close his eyes. Suggest to him how wonderful it would be to drift off to somewhere.

You: *I wonder if you can imagine a place where you can let go... Somewhere nice... Where you can lay comfortably... You're floating off... Wherever you wish to go... Somewhere nice... Think of your arms... they're feeling heavy... Imagine your legs... they're feeling heavy...Just let it go... Imagine leaving your legs behind as you float...Float away...*

- Then, pull the subject deeper into the trance by describing to him how he is relaxing even more.

You: *Imagine that you're inside a room... Inside that room is a staircase leading downwards... You can descend these stairs... It is safe... It is comfortable... And you are carried down... down... downwards... And you are feeling more relaxed... With every step you take... down... your body grows more relaxed... your mind grows more relaxed...*

- Begin the countdown induction by telling the subject that that he is descending towards ten steps.

You: *10... You're going deeper... 9... You are more relaxed... 8... deeper... 7... and deeper... 6... and deeper...*

When you reach one, tell the subject that he is wandering off towards a warm and welcoming place.

- At this point, you are to tell the subject to open his eyes but suggest that he is unable to open them. This is done to ensure that he has truly been hypnotized.

You: *Place your attention towards your eyes... Imagine that they've become so relaxed... So tired... So tightly shut... That you cannot open them...You try to open them, but it won't work...It won't work...*

- Then, instruct the subject to open his eyes. If he is unable to, then he is in hypnosis. But if he is able to, then it simply means that the person requires a different hypnosis technique. Keep in mind that when done correctly, a state of trance can be achieved by most people in less than a couple of minutes. Another sign that the technique has worked is if you see the subject's eyes flickering or his fingers twitching. Perform a finger lift because this test is difficult to fake.

You: *Now, you are feeling your hands... Let your mind think about your hands... How much it weights... Its temperature... Its sensation... You are aware that your mind has a need to move your hand... any part... any finger... Let your mind do it... On its own... Just let it happen...*

Observe the response. An immediate movement or lift of a finger or the hand means that the individual is faking it. A genuine response would be a small movement.

- Once you are sure that the subject is in a trance, deepen their hypnosis.

You: *Good... good... It's how it should be... I wonder if you can think of yourself sitting on a comfortable chair... Relaxing... Breathing... Doing nothing... Thinking of nothing... Worrying about nothing...*

Say something affirming and keep reassuring the subject.

- You may now proceed to influencing his thoughts as well as his behavior.

You: *Imagine all the endless possibilities while you are in this state... the vivid way in which you can imagine things... recall things... become aware of things... all things within... and without... as though you are drifting... Open... Free...*

Whatever suggestion you have planned for the subject, now it the time to plant it.

- Finally, you may bring the person out of hypnosis. During the entire process, you are expected to watch the individual's breathing very closely. Each suggestion must be delivered in time with his breathing. You are to speak as the subject exhales and then you wait for him to inhale.

You: *Now, it's time for you to come back to the present... I am going to count from five to one, and when I reach one... You will return... You will be awake... Five... Four... Three... Two... One.*

Chapter 6

Progressive Relaxation Induction

The Progressive Relaxation Induction, also known as the Jacobson relaxation technique, is considered as the simplest and easiest method. Hence, it is recommended for beginners. The following is a sample Progressive Muscle Relaxation (PMR) hypnosis induction script. Keep in mind that you don't necessarily have to read out from the script. In fact, it would be much better if you can practice it beforehand. You don't need to memorize the words because they merely exist as a guide and you can easily change them. Your focus should be on the flow.

Be sure to deliver your words gently. Don't use a commanding tone on the subject. Also, make sure that you are watching the person closely and don't forget to provide affirmation and reassurance. As with the instructions for basic hypnosis, you are to speak and plant your suggestions each time the individual exhales. Deliver your words gently but not too slowly because this allows the person to have time to analyze words as opposed to automatically acting on your suggestions. In using this method, the best way to bring the subject deeper is through silence.

➢ The Pre-talk

- The first step would be to ask the person to find a comfortable position. He may either sit of lie down. It would be better if he is wearing relaxed garments. Otherwise, be sure to loosen any tight clothing. The shoes may be removed and the person's pockets may be emptied of any bulky items.

- Then, utilize metaphor by saying something like: *Kindly ensure that your phone has already gone into SLEEP mode...*

- Seed ideas by telling the subject what you're going to speak to him about. Tell him that you'll be talking to him about relaxation. Tell him that this will enable his mind to drift away.

- Provide reassurance by telling the subject that hypnosis is a safe and pleasant experience. Let him know that while a part of him is in trance, a part of him will also remain aware. Let him know that he will be able to emerge from the trance anytime he chooses. Ensure him that he will be safe and that what you'll be doing is for his own good. Let him know that he is in control of the situation. Tell him that he may move any time he wishes in order to be comfortable and that he may reject and forget any words that you might say that makes him feel uncomfortable.

- Bind the subject permissively by asking him to close his eyes. Ask permission to touch one or both of his wrists while he is in a trance.

➢ The Breathing Induction

- You: *Allow yourself to be relaxed... Once you are comfortable, feel back of the chair... think of how well it supports your back... of how well it supports you... Close your eyes...*

By saying this, you are creating a lenient bind.

- Ask the subject to take a deep breath and then to hold that breath. Tell him that when he exhales, he should allow his body to relax.

You: *That's it... Relax...*

By using this, you are influencing the person's natural parasympathetic response.

- Now, it's time to ask the person to take a second breath. Ask him to relieve the tension in his body with his exhalation.

- Then, ask him to take the third deep breath. And with this breath, he releases all of the existing tension.

You: *Let your head, your arms, and your legs go limp. Like a cloth draped lazily across a chair...*

By saying this, you are making use of metaphor and visualization.

- Utilize the power of presupposition and increase the subject's capability by saying this.

You: *Your body is relaxed... Very relaxed... Still, surprisingly, you'll find out how much more relaxed it can be... So very relaxed... Ten times more relaxed than it already is...*

➢ **Progressive Muscle Relaxation**

- By this time, you are to instruct the person to concentrate his attention on his eyes and on all the small muscles that constitute his eyelids. Remind him that he has full control over all those tiny muscles.

You: *I wonder if you can picture your eyes growing so relaxed... So relaxed... And once you are sure that they are... let that feeling of relaxation reach your forehead... all the small muscles in your forehead smoothened out...*

- Then, instruct them to do the same thing with their cheeks.

You: *I wonder if you can feel the muscles on your cheeks relaxing...flattening...*

- Guide the subject so that the sensation of relaxation is felt in the jaw, his mouth, his lips, his entire face...

- If the subject is indeed, following your suggestion, then you will notice some slight movement around the jaw. His head will noticeably relax.

- Then, guide the feeling of relaxation so that it travels down the neck and to the shoulders. Create a sensory distortion by telling the subject that he will feel limp and heavy once he shrugs and releases his shoulders.

- Move towards the chest and allow the subject to feel his spine, his abdominal area, and all the parts connected to them relaxing.

You: *Imagine how well these parts of you can relax... and how with each passing second, they can relax more... and more...*

An important note: Never mention the heart.

- Then, move towards the arms. Create a sense of dissociation from the body by asking the subject to tense the muscles in his arms and then to let go of it and its weight.

You: *Feel how heavy your arms are... And how, when you let go of them, the weight has gone away... the arms have gone away... far, far away... like they're not yours anymore...*

➢ **The Depth Test**

- Inform the subject that you are going to touch his wrist and then lift his right hand.

You: *While I am doing this, you may keep on relaxing... deeper... You don't have to pay attention to me... or to your arm... and when I lift it, it will drop like a wet towel... I am now lifting your arm...*

This is called the arm flop test used to determine the depth of the trance. It is necessary to warn the subject at all times before touching him. Touch the person's wrist by its bony knob. Note that when you move the arm, it should not bend at the shoulder. This shows resistance. Instead, it should bend at the elbow.

You: *I am about to let go of your wrist... When I do this, you will feel yourself being more relaxed... and going deeper... safer... warmer... and deeper...*

You should be able to feel that the arm is heavy and it should drop like a dead weight. Otherwise, this suggests that the subject is not yet in a state of hypnosis. The best result that a hypnotist can hope for is when the person's arm is dropped and that it stays in the air momentarily until it moves down.

- Perform a second arm drop by touching the person's left wrist. Again, be sure to warn him. This time you are supposed to give the left wrist a small tug while you lift it. Then you are to let go of the wrist immediately, just enough to surprise the person. While the subject's left arm is falling be sure to say the following in a firmer tone: *And now deeper... and deeper... down... down...* then, provide affirmation.

You: *That's good... Let go... Let the relaxation flow to each and every muscle in your body...*

- If you are sure that the person is now in a trance, you may begin planting your suggestion. Otherwise, you may move towards the legs. Create the same sense of dissociation like what you have just done with the arms. Create the feeling that he is separated from his arms and his legs.

Eventually, the person will feel relaxed so that he will forget about almost everything. At that point, it should be difficult for him to find the energy to do anything. When you are done stating your suggestion and reinforcing it with supporting statements, wake the subject from the trance gradually.

Chapter 7

Hypnosis Using the Eyes and Visualization Hypnotherapy

Hypnosis Using the Eyes

- Before you attempt to hypnotize a person using your eyes, you must first practice eye focusing exercises. Try to maintain prolonged periods of eye contact without even blinking. Start by staring into your own eyes in the mirror. Use a timer to find out how long you can last without straying or blinking. You can also perform this exercise with another person.

- Practice your eyes' focus flexibility by holding a pencil close to your face and by focusing on it. Then, direct your gaze from the pencil to an object in the farther end of the room. Focus your attention there. Then, direct your gaze back towards the pencil. Again, move your concentration to the same distant object. Keep doing this.

- Another ability that you must improve is your peripheral awareness. Select a busy environment for your practice like a park or the marketplace. Try to observe the people and their movements with your head turned to the left side. Then, move your head to the right side. Again, try to observe the busy scene. Make an attempt to catch every possible movement that you can. Continue practicing.

- When you're ready to hypnotize someone with your eyes, be sure to ask for the person's permission. The subject must be a willing participant. Then, have him sit in a comfortable position. Or he may stand erect. Make sure that the subject is not slouching and his body weight should be evenly distributed.

- Then, ask the subject to concentrate his gaze on the spot beneath your right eye. Tell him not to look away. At this point, you are not allowed to blink.

- Then, as you keep staring into the subject's eyes, begin counting down from five to one using a low and soothing tone.

5

Your eyelids are feeling heavy.

4

They are feeling heavier and heavier.

3

Soon, you will feel that your eyelids are so heavy, they will begin to close.

2

The more you try to move your eyelids, the more you try to open them, the more they will feel heavy and the more they will close...

1

Keep repeating the phrases but remember to present them in a different manner each time. In short, learn how to paraphrase.

- Then, inform the subject that you are going to touch his shoulder. Tell him that as you touch his shoulder, it will become floppy. Whatever you do to the subject, you must inform him of it. This is a way of setting up his mind for your command.

- Then, touch the person's shoulder and perform the arm flop test similar to the techniques in the previous chapters. The shoulder must drop limply when you touch it.

Reassure the subject.

- Once you have confirmed that the person is under hypnosis, he is now ready to listen to your voice.

Count down again from five to one.

Five...

Four...

Three...

Two...

Tell the subject that when you reach one, he will only be able to hear the sound of your voice.

One.

Snap your fingers as you reach one.

Say this: *Allow my voice to relax you deeper and deeper... Hear every word that I say and hear ONLY the words that I say.*

- It is now time to embed a suggestion or a command.

Visualization Hypnotherapy

Visualization hypnotherapy is an easy technique which utilizes the subject's imagination. It builds a process where the person is able to move through the situation that has been causing his problems. The mind will not be able to differentiate between what is real and what is not. Consider visualization as a form of mental rehearsal that will affect the individual's actions when he emerges from hypnosis.

Some people have trouble with visualizing on demand. In some cases, they need to perform a few visualization exercises.

Orange Visualization Exercise

Imagine that you're sitting in a garden.

You're sitting on the grass.

Beside you is a picnic basket.

Imagine yourself opening that picnic basket.

Inside the basket are oranges.

You reach out and select a nice orange.

You feel its roundness and its weight in your hand.

You slide your fingers over the orange's skin. It feels smooth and waxy.

You can feel the orange's texture beneath your thumb.

Then, you lift the orange to your face and inhale its sweet citrus scent.

You slice the orange open.

The bright orange flesh is exposed and you see the juice dribble from it.

You cut a slice of the orange then you place it in your mouth.

You bite down on its juicy flesh and the nectar runs over your tongue.

It fills your mouth with a sweet citrus taste.

Most subjects will feel their mouth watering after this exercise because in order for these words to work, the subconscious has to access memories. It will retrieve memories associated with oranges, allowing the person to recall the colors, the smells, the taste and the textures associated with eating an orange and this can create a strong physical reaction.

During visualization hypnosis, the visualization is used to reinforce the hypnotist's suggestion. For example, a person wishes to stop smoking. Create a scenario for him where he is offered a cigarette but then he refuses it. If the subject wishes to gain self-confidence, then place him in a social setting where he can see himself engaging in conversation and feeling at ease with other people. An individual with an eating disorder can be asked to see himself in a banquet where he chooses only healthy food. If a person feels a stabbing pain in his abdomen, use visualization to create a cushion around that area that stops the stabbing sensation.

Be sure to visualize only positive things. This can also be used in self-hypnosis to make yourself feel happier, more successful, or to help you break free from a bad habit.

Chapter 8

Hypnosis and Weight Loss

One of the most recent forms of hypnosis has something to do with weight loss.

A perfect example of this would be Marion Corns, a woman from the United Kingdom who underwent Hypnosis to believe that she has undergone Gastric Bypass Surgery. By believing in this, she learned how to control the amount she's eating. While she used to eat as many plates of food as she wanted, she now only eats small portions. This is because she believes that her stomach shrunk to the size of a golf ball!

According to her, she has tried a lot of diet plans before but none of them really worked as she would just go back to her old habits, but because she now believes that a gastric bypass has been done, she tells herself not to eat too much anymore.

What's amazing, too, is the fact that she really didn't undergo gastric bypass, and yet, she's able to reap the benefits. An operation would have cost her a little more than $7,000. She didn't actually shelve out that cash, but now, she has lost a lot of pounds—and that's all because of Hypnosis!

She underwent five sessions of gastric hypnosis in a hospital in Spain. She was already supposed to go through the operation there, but then she found out that that the clinic also gives Gastric Hypnosis sessions, so she decided to go for that one. After 5 sessions, she felt like her stomach was tightening, and every time she tries to eat more than she should, she just feels like she's going to throw up.

According to her, what happened was that she went through Cognitive Behavioral Therapy, which could also be a form of hypnosis. Now, she feels like she finally fits in with society, and she no longer feels like she has to hide from people.

Gastric Hypnosis, as well as Weight Loss Hypnosis, in general, is great for overweight teens and adults. It's said that it is now changing the face of weight loss programs not only in United Kingdom, but in the whole world, as well. This is because people learn how to be more disciplined—and they also learn to understand that they can lose weight even without using too much cash, as long as they know how to control themselves.

Hypnosis is not a miraculous cure to weight problems. It is actually a complex process. For instance, you cannot just hypnotize someone into eating less. If that person eats less, then his energy would drop. He'd have less energy to move about. If he isn't physically active, his metabolism will be at risk of slowing down, which will eventually result to the body burning lesser amount of fat. It's counterproductive since one has to lose fat in order to lose unwanted weight. Hypnosis for weight loss requires an overall approach.

So how exactly does it work?

Because hypnosis can affect a person's unconscious motivations, patterns and feelings, it can be used effectively to help someone who deals with weight problems. The key is to change the way of thinking. For instance, we eat because food tastes good and because it is necessary for survival. However, we often forget about the importance of eating mindfully and healthily. When we begin to feel that we want to consume food in a healthy manner then it will change everything.

Hypnosis works in a way that it can be used to help someone naturally feel that he is making the right choice when it comes to food. Does this mean taking away someone's willpower? It doesn't. What it simply means is helping someone feel better about using his willpower as far as food choices are concerned.

Losing weight after all, is not about getting rid of something we do not want or need. People have become so focused on exercise routines and obsessed with 'healthy' foods. It is of course, perfectly alright to pay attention to these things but it is also important to train our brains. That is where hypnosis comes in.

Hypnosis can help in such a way that a person can create a new relationship with his body and with food. Rather than taking away someone's willpower, hypnosis can be used successfully to reinforce someone's power to choose and be more honest with these choices. For instance, you know you can always have chocolate cake and you can have as much as you want but do you really have to have it? You know you want it but do you really need it?

There are various approaches to using hypnosis for weight loss. Do not simply focus on one aspect. Choose a set of approaches relevant to that person.

- Use suggestions to help the person envision the body he wants and the level of health and fitness he wants to achieve.
- Use positive suggestions to help someone maximize his motivation to eat healthily.
- Encourage the person to level up his fat-burning metabolism. Provide certain cues that will remind him to exercise. For instance, you can suggest that at a specific time of each day, his legs will feel restless, which means it is time to exercise.
- Metaphors can also be used successfully. For example, you can conjure up an image in the person's mind of a sculptor facing a shapeless rock. In order to uncover the real form of that rock, the sculptor must work on it little by little, carefully and patiently. When the real form is revealed, he can get rid of the excess and needless rocks.

- Another imagery you can use to help someone lose weight is to guide him into visualizing that he is wearing a fat suit. Guide him into imagining that he is able to discard layers from his fat suit. Reinforce that feeling of relief as he removes one layer at a time until the suit is in the 'right' size, the way he wants his body to look like.

- Help the person focus not just on numbers and weight but also on health and fitness.

- Help the person make a distinction between real food and fake food, the ones that are good for him and the ones that aren't.

- Use hypnotic journey metaphor. Suggest that in each step of the journey, he feels lighter and better about himself. Allow him to think about what he's wearing as he gets farther in the journey.

- Use disassociation to help this person see himself in the future when he eats well, exercises regularly, looking slimmer and feeling much lighter.

- Use age progression. Take him into the future where he has become slimmer. Suggest that he goes back in time from the future and remember exactly what he needed to do to make this happen and how easy and effortless it was.

- Help the person realize that when he exercises more, his will to exercise becomes greater and it becomes much easier.

➢ Help him remember that when he feels the desire to eat unhealthy or consume food when he is not hungry, he is not reaching his goal. Let him imagine how it will make him feel to not reach his goal.

Here's a sample script.

Close your eyes and relax. Notice how tension is released from your body at each breath, from the top of your head, easing your facial muscles to your nape and neck. As you continue to breathe slowly, feel the way it eases your shoulders, arms and fingers. Now the calming energy travels from your chest to your abdomen, from your pelvic area down to your legs, feet and toes. You are no completely relaxed. You are free.

Now see yourself standing and walking forward. Your naked feet touch the moist and green grass. Notice how refreshing that feels. Notice the feeling of gaining momentum at each step you take forward. Feel that progression. Look up and see the light shining down on your path, guiding you in the right direction.

As you move one foot after the other, you are getting close to finding out where this path is taking you. That's it, slowly and steadily, you are progressing. In a few moments, you will see a mirror along this path. You see it now. You can see your reflection. I wonder if you can see your reflection changing as you move closer. Can you see your figure getting slimmer and slimmer as you walk towards the mirror? You're feeling light on your feet.

Feel the space around you change as you become slimmer and slimmer. Do you notice the beautiful colors around you? The grass is greener and flowers bloom. The breeze kisses your skin and the warm sun shines comfortably. The birds are singing. Feel everything around you. You're getting nearer in a month's time. That's it... Now, you can clearly see it. It is not just your imagination. You are finding your real shape... That's it... At the back of your mind, you can continue walking to this path even when you are not consciously aware of it.

Now, let's drift into the future six months time. Think about what you're wearing. Notice how you're feeling with your real shape. Can you imagine how it feels to have uncovered your real shape? Notice how good it feels. You feel much lighter and comfortable. You can move easier. You look younger and more attractive.

Looking back at those six months now, think about the things you needed to do to reach this point, to discover your real shape. Could you think about how easy it was to become slimmer naturally? Take a few moments to reflect on these things from the future, feeling so much better about yourself in this way...

That's it... Now you can drift back to the present. Slowly open your eyes and feel nicer and more alert...

To reinforce the sessions, you can also suggest for this person to recite the following positive affirmations.

I am focused on my goal. I stay focused on the shape that I deserve. It is all about each meal that I take.

I am twice as active every day.

I burn excess fat with each step that I take. I have no urge to eat fake foods.

I drink water in between meals. I feel nourished.

I am tomorrow because of what I eat and do today.

Here are some of the things you have to keep in mind if you want to use hypnosis for weight loss:

1. **You need a lot of practice**. Even Marion Corns says that it wasn't always easy for her, especially during the first few days after the end of the Gastric Hypnosis sessions. But then, she would just remind herself that she no longer has a lot of space in her stomach, and that she could only eat small amounts of food—and that's what she focused on, instead of all the temptations around her. As with anything else in life, once you concentrate on this—even for just 15 to 20 minutes a day, it'll already make a world of difference.

2. **It takes a lot of behavioral modification.** According to one of the most popular hypnotists of all time, Dr. Milton

Erickson, said that it is extremely important to help yourself modify your behavior, and that it's essential to use existing patterns. He says that while you're at your heaviest, you have to think of your highest calorie craving. For example, think of the sweetest kind of ice cream, but don't buy some. Instead, choose to have yogurt instead.

So, basically, you have to think of the alternatives. You have to think of other food products you can eat to satisfy your cravings. Also, it would be nice if you could look at an old photo of yourself—a photo of you when you are at your fattest. Then, look at a photo of someone you want to emulate—and focus on that. Remind yourself that you want to be the person on the second photo, so that you can twist your mind in such a way that it would help your body work to achieve what you want.

3. **Think Positive.** Okay. It totally sounds like a cliché, but the thing is when it comes to hypnosis, you cannot allow yourself to think negatively. Even saying things such as *too much ice cream will damage you* is NOT good. Instead, you can say something like *my body does not need too many calories. I need to take care of myself.* You always have to remind yourself why you are doing this, and why you have to be disciplined. That's a better way of helping yourself achieve what you want, instead of focusing on the negative.

4. **Trust Yourself.** According to most gastric hypnotists, this is basically the most important thing. You have to believe in yourself in order for you to lose weight. If you don't, you're already on the first step to downfall. Just practice until the process of believing in yourself becomes innate to you—and you'd lose weight in no time!

Chapter 9

Hypnosis against Stress

Everyone probably experiences stress at some level in their lives. Nearly half of the adult population suffers from its adverse effects. Among these effects include anxiety, depression, arthritis, asthma, high blood pressure, skin conditions, heart problems and headaches. 75 to 90 percent of doctor visits are because of stress-related issues. When chronic stress is untreated, it can lead to emotional disorder.

Life could really get so stressful, and these days, it's important to find ways to relieve stress without using too much money, or creating more hassle.

One of these ways is hypnotherapy. Research has it that hypnotherapy is one of the best ways of relieving stress, especially for children and teens dealing with anxiety issues. It is said that with the help of hypnosis, feelings of helplessness are lessened, and that it's proven to be even greater than that of other traditional relaxation techniques.

It is actually common for kids aged 11 to 15 to develop and experience signs of panic attacks and anxiety. If one wants these experiences to be lessened, he has to learn how to target them right away, then one should at least try going through hypnosis.

Start them early

According to Ian Goodyer, a Professor of Child and Adolescent Psychiatry from Cambridge University said that when anxiety is not treated head on, children would develop avoidance behaviors, and may also become hypersensitive because they're not able to understand what's going on with them.

However, when a child becomes acquainted with cognitive behavioral training and hypnosis early on, it will be easier for him to understand himself. Furthermore, this would also help kids understand that their behaviors should not make them ashamed, but help themselves realize that they could still do better, and that it's not too late yet.

When one undergoes hypnosis, he begins to learn how to control himself, as well as his thoughts and feelings, which of course, would eventually ease the feelings of anxiety and panic—and any other kinds of pain he's been dealing with. Parents will also begin to see positive changes in their kids' behaviors when this happens, too.

Parents and children should work together

Meanwhile, according to David Byron, a Senior Specialist from the Hampshire County Council, parents have to be open to hypnosis, too. After all, they'll be the ones who need to learn hypnotherapy techniques so they could apply those on their children.

In short, if they do not have open minds and hearts for this, it probably would not work the way they want it to.

While some parents are still keen on doing traditional practices, it's been proven that those who were willing to try hypnosis, and those who studied hypnotism were able to rear their children the right way. Their kids now have more chances of growing up confident and strong, and are well-empowered, as well.

Stress can be triggered by various factors but no matter what the triggers are, it is the mind that is in control of how the body responds to these triggers. If we think of a situation as stressful then our body follows and responds to it accordingly. With the help of hypnotherapy, we can change how our minds interpret these situations. Rather than stressing out, we can learn to stay calm and more relaxed. We do not have to feel helpless. We can stay in control under circumstances when we normally feel like we are not. If our mind learns to interpret "stressful" situations in a different way, we can significantly reduce stress in our lives and we can feel lighter, happier and healthier.

How it happens

When it comes to using hypnosis to alleviate stress, the first thing that you have to put in mind is that it has a lot to do with *Creative Visualization*, and *Positive Stimulation.*

What happens here is that you get to stimulate the immune system in a positive manner. Through this, negative self-image is released, and one would be able to pursue his goals clearer, and find ways to achieve them fast. Emotional, physical, and mental stress are also relieved because of this, and subsequently, stress-related illnesses, such as insomnia and high blood pressure, too!

Basically, with positive stimulation, you get to do the following:

1. **Stress Management.** You get to the root of the problem so that one day, you could finally move on from it.

2. **Confidence.** When you know what's bothering you, you also begin to know yourself better. And when you know yourself better, you become more confident and at peace with yourself.

3. **Communication Skills.** Now, when you are at peace with yourself, you also learn how to mingle with other people. See, the thing with people who suffer from anxiety is that more often than not, they feel like they could no longer relate to people, and they have no idea how to blurt out what they want. But, when they learn who they are, they tend to understand how to put themselves out there again, and how to tell people about themselves, and about what they want, as well. In short, they begin to see the beauty of being around other people again.

4. **Performance Anxiety.** Performance anxiety is also tackled. When one undergoes hypnosis, he gets to be more confi-

dent about himself again that he would no longer have problems talking to a large group of people (i.e., during recitation, talent shows, presentations, group meetings, etc.) and so, he would learn how to harness his talents more so that he can make use of them more in the future!

5. **Focus.** When one is confident about himself and is not riddled by anxiety, he tends to focus better, too. And of course, when one focuses better, it's just imperative that the quality of work he's able to provide would also be the best!

6. **Clear Thinking.** Finally, going through positive stimulation would lead to a clear mind—what else is better than that?

You can do this any time of the day. What matters is that you learn how to make it a part of your daily life—even just five minutes of your day would already be enough!

Here's what you can do:

1. Go to a quiet place. It could either be a room, or your backyard—as long as you're alone then that will do.

2. Then, close your eyes and take measured, deep breaths. Think of your surroundings, and imagine that they're the most beautiful things you've seen in life; or, think about a place that you want to visit, and that makes you feel good inside.

3. Let all the elements of that scene in your head come to life. For example: the feel of grass on your toes, the smell of flowers around you, the blue sky, the wind on your face, etc.

4. Think about how you feel while you're in the place you have described in your head. Do you feel warm? Do you feel cool? Does it make you feel better inside?

5. Stay focused on the said image for at least five minutes.

Repeat as necessary.

Consistency is key

Remember, it's essential to be consistent and to do positive stimulation every day for it to work. It's one of the simplest forms of hypnosis that you can do—so make sure you do it well.

Here's a sample script. You can use it on someone else or record your voice reading it for self-hypnosis.

Close your eyes and relax. Notice how tension is released from your body at each breath, from the top of your head, easing your facial muscles to your nape and neck. As you continue to breathe slowly, feel the way it eases your shoulders and jaw down to your arms and fingers. Now the calming energy travels from your chest to your abdomen, from your pelvic area down to your legs, feet and toes. You are no completely relaxed. You are free.

Everything feels soft and comfortable like you are being wrapped up in a soft, warm blanket. As you relax more, you feel much more at ease. If you can go deeper, you feel much better. If you can feel better, you go much deeper. That's right...

You are beginning to feel a sense of appreciation, confidence and happiness. Every inch of your body is relaxed. Your mind is at ease. This is how it feels to rest peacefully, to unwind. You can have this every day. You deserve to feel this way.

From this moment forward, you are relaxed and calm. You are able to deal with any situation in a positive way. This feeling of calmness, of positivity grows stronger within you. It becomes a real part of you each day. This positive idea of calmness is what you want in your life. And you welcome it with open arms.

From this moment forward, the things that have caused trouble in your life, those things that have brought you anxiety and stress... no longer affect you in the same way. You feel them wash away, leaving you at peace, at ease, calm.

As you relax more, as you breathe deeper and slower, these suggestions grow stronger. They become more real to you. That's it...

In a few moments, I will count to three. Think about one particular thing that generally causes you stress or tension. As you think about it, I want you to make a fist. I wonder if you could you squeeze the tension out of you? Use positivity and calmness to drive away that thought. One... Two... Three... Think about that something. Now make a fist and picture yourself squeezing out the tension. You're squeezing out the stress, the worries and anxiety into that fist.

I want you to repeat this word after me. Say them slowly... Relax...

From this moment forward, when you say the word "relax," you release the tension and stress. You allow your muscles, every part of your body to completely relax. You welcome a feeling of calmness. Notice how wonderful it feels right now. You will always remember this wonderful and positive feeling when you say the word "relax." When you say "relax," you remember to look at and deal with situations in a positive way because you are a calm and positive person. Because this is what you want in your life, you want to be at peace, at ease and calm.

One... Two... Three... "Relax..."

As you say the word "relax" more often, its positive effect grows stronger and better.

Release the fist... You are completely calm, at peace and at ease. You are positive and you respond to situations in a positive way.

One... Two... Three... "Relax..."

Just saying the word makes you feel good physically. It eases your mind. The feeling of calmness becomes more real. You welcome this feeling of relaxation.

One... Two... Three... "Relax..."

From this moment forward, when you are facing a situation that would normally make you feel stressed out and tensed. Make a fist and imagine squeezing the anxiety out, picture yourself squeezing the stress and tension into your fist. And when you say quietly to yourself, "relax," you feel a wave of calmness and relaxation wash over you. You feel positivity filling you up. You completely relax.

You feel calmer each day... You feel more relaxed right now. You feel more positive and it transcends to everything you do... You feel more confident because you feel more in control... You feel a great feeling of well being... You feel wonderful physically and mentally because this is what you want in your life. It means you want to be positive always. And you allow yourself to be...

That's it... Now on the count of three, you can drift back to the present. Slowly open your eyes. You feel nicer, calmer and more positive. Open your eyes with a smile. Allow the positive energy to come out from within you. One... Two... Three...

You can read this to yourself or to someone or simply use this as a guide to make your own, so you can be stress-free and help someone else become free of stress as well.

Chapter 10

Hypnosis and Pain Management

If hypnosis can relieve stress, you can also expect that it can manage pain, too.

According to a study done by the Journal of National Cancer Institute, breast cancer patients who have to undergo operations tend to need fewer anesthetics when they've gone through hypnosis, even in different forms. More so, the patients have also agreed that side effects, such as headaches, fatigue, and nausea are no longer that evident because of hypnosis.

Money is saved

Another great benefit of having patients undergo hypnosis is that both the patient and the hospital get to save money. According to Dr. David Speigel of Stanford University, it all stems from the fact that with the help of hypnosis, people tend to pay more attention to the pain they're feeling.

That may sound confusing, but here's how it goes: when you pay attention to how you are feeling, you know that you'd get hurt. When you know that you'd get hurt, you can tell yourself that you can look forward to feeling healed after. Basically, hypnosis turns the negative effects of pain on the body to positive ones because your perception is transformed.

Hence, money used for pain medication and therapies that one has to go through after operations would be lessened, and the person would feel so much better inside. This is because hypnosis is able to change pain experience even better than placebos and analgesics.

What you can do

1. **Breathing Exercises.** There are various kinds of these, but do start with the ones below:

    a. **Progressive Relaxation**. Close your eyes to nix tension from head to toe. Tense and relax each muscle group for at least 2 to 3 seconds before moving. It would be best to start with your feet, all the way to the eyes. Hold for a count of five, and then breathe out using the mouth.

    b. **Skull Shining Breath/Kapalabhati.** Inhale in a long and slow motion, then use your lower belly to exhale forcefully. Inhale every 1 to 2 seconds from the nose, and repeat for at least 10 breaths. Do this upon waking up, or early in the morning.

    c. **Alternate Nostril Breathing.** It is said that this exercise is meant to bring balance and calmness to the person going through it. Do this while in a meditative pose. Hold your right thumb over the right nostril, and use left nostril to inhale. Use ring finger to close left nostril, and then use right nostril to exhale. Use right nostril to continue doing so, and close left nostril with left thumb after.

d. **Abdominal Breathing Technique.** This is best done before presentations, or when you're feeling stressed because of pain. Put one hand over your chest and the other over your belly, and use the nose to take a deep breath. Stretch some air in the lungs using the diaphragm, and do at least 6 to 10 deep breaths for at least 10 minutes each day in a matter of 6 weeks.

e. **Equal Breathing/Samma Vriti.** This technique is said to be best done shortly before going to bed. Inhale for four counts, and exhale for another four. Once you've gotten the hang of it, you can do around 6 to 8 breaths. Think of this as a way of counting sheep, if you have trouble going to sleep.

2. **Autogenic Training.** Relaxation is achieved with the use of body awareness and visual imagery. You can either do this by yourself, or while being guided by a therapist. What happens here is that you take deep breaths while focusing on various physical sensations, so you could cope with life stressors, especially in the future.

Autogenic Training doesn't come easy, though. Just like any kind of hypnosis, it takes a lot of practice. Here are the things that you could do to get better at it:

a. Make sure that you're alone and you are in a quiet place.

b. Make sure there is no music or background noise around.

c. Wear loose clothing, and make sure to remove your shoes.

d. Avoid drinking, eating, or smoking before going to practice. Also, don't ever practice when you have taken medicine.

e. If you feel so sleepy, or have actually fallen asleep during the session, practice another time when you're awake and in the mood, instead.

f. For a few seconds after practice, close your eyes and slowly get up. This way, you'd notice blood pressure ascend for a bit. You could also try counting backwards (10 to 1 or 5 to 1), so your eyes would be fully alert and supremely calm.

g. It's not recommended that you practice in bed, but if you want to do so, make sure that you fall asleep right after. This way, your mind would associate autogenic training to being in a state of peace (i.e., falling asleep) and so it would work better.

h. Remember to focus on your inner experiences as opposed to external events. Focus on what you feel inside, not on what's happening outside. This will teach you to ignore things that will actually just come to pass.

3. **Transcendal Meditation.** Transcendal meditation is intended to help you avoid distracting thoughts, and in turn bring you to a state of relaxed awareness. The key is to close your eyes and think of a mantra. Of course, the mantra has to be positive so that the negative emotions will come to pass. Sometimes, the mantra could also come from your instructor, so that mental boundaries would be set.

   You can join transcendal meditation classes to make sure that you understand how it works. What happens is that the transcendal meditation (TM) instructor explains to you the information about the technique for at least 60 minutes. Then, you go to another lecture which would then last for around 45 minutes, and then you'd attend an interview which you'd spend at least 10 to 15 minutes in. After the said interview, you'd receive 1 to 2 hours of personal instruction. It kind of sounds long, but just be patient because it definitely is for your own good.

   Then, the ceremony begins and you'd be given your own mantra. Take note that this has to be done in private, and you should not give up the mantra for public consumption.

   Then, in a matter of 3 days, you will be checked for correctness, and it would be followed up by at least 1 to 2 more hours of instruction. During this phase, you can expect the instructor to:

a. Explain some more about transcendal meditation, and provide you with necessary corrections.

b. Tell you why it's important to practice regularly.

c. Then, you can expect the sessions to go on for the next couple of months, and for you to be able to get the hang of it.

Take note that TM should be done for 15 to 20 minutes, twice a day. It would be best to do so before breakfast, and before dinner. Also, just remember to relax. You do not have to exert strenuous effort, and you don't have to tire yourself out for this.

Here's a sample script you can use as a reference or to read to yourself or to someone suffering from pain. You can record and listen to this script along with the exercises suggested above.

You are now completely calm and relaxed... deeper and deeper you go... the more comfortable you become... You open yourself up and willingly receive these rewarding suggestions. Your thoughts may drift away but your subconscious is completely attentive. Your subconscious is open and welcoming to these suggestions I will now offer you...

I wonder if you could imagine being in a wonderful beach. Could you see the calm see? Could you feel the sun shining down on your? Could you feel the warm breeze kissing your skin? Could you imagine how good it feels, the quietness, the calmness, everything around you is relaxed and at peace. You can hear the sound of the waves, the sound of water washing over the warm sand... The water almost touches your feet... It feels so good, so relaxing. Everything around you is calm. You are comfortable and relaxed...

Now you see an empty bottle washed ashore. It rests in front of you. I want you to pick it up. That's it... Feel it. Hold it... Look at it... It's corked, old and empty. You can open it. Open it effortlessly... That's it...

Now I would like you to use the strength of your subconscious and the power of imagination to fill the bottle with your pain, pour all your pain into the empty bottle. Allow the pain to flow from your body and into the bottle. It flows... It is slowly filling up the bottle... That's it... Let the pain leave your body and flow into the bottle... Let it all out... Let it all flow... The bottle is big enough to contain all the pain so pour everything into the bottle. Let go of your pain... That's it... Now all your pain has flowed out from your body and into the bottle, you can see your pain inside the bottle. I want you to put the cork back into the bottle to lock away all the pain inside it. Muster all your strength and throw the bottle into the water. Throw it as far as you can. That's right...

As the bottle floats into the water, as it goes farther and farther away, your pain goes with it. Away and away, farther and farther it goes. All your pain has gone away with the bottle and it is now farther and farther away from you. Watch it float away in the current. Keep watching it until it floats and fades away into the abyss...

In a few moments, I want you take three deep breaths. I will now count to three. Ready... 1... Breathe in deeply, hold it in for a few moments... now breathe out slowly... The pain is gone. You are free from pain. You are completely comfortable and relaxed... 2... You poured all your pain into that bottle and it's not gone, the pain is all gone, gone with the bottle... 3... You feel joyful... You feel calm and happy... You feel strong... You feel healthy...

Chapter 11

Hypnosis and Synesthesia

Interestingly enough, hypnosis also induces synesthesia.

You know how using pot or LSD is often associated with tasting or hearing colors? That's basically what synesthesia is about, and hypnosis can bring forth the same effects!

According to most researchers, most infants are born with sensory regions in their brain connected. Synthesis then happens on those regions, and kids are able to recognize that, but once they've been trained to see colors as one particular thing (i.e., yellow is yellow; colors are not tangible, etc.), of course, their brain gets twisted in this way, too. So, there's a tendency that synthesis gets lost while the child is growing.

Have you ever heard of the saying that apparently, kids could see ghosts and other unseen beings when they're still infants or toddlers? That's the probable reason why they tend to have "imaginary friends", too.

It's almost the same with synesthesia. While the person's natural ability to create synesthesia is lost, it could still be tapped in a natural manner—in short, by means of hypnosis!

Colors and Sounds

In studies done by the University College of London and University of Murcia in Spain, people who were put in hypnosis were instructed to see digits in color (i.e., one = red, two = blue, three = yellow, etc). When the subjects woke up, they then found it hard to recognize the numbers when they're printed in black and white, but they were able to recognize them when they were printed in the colors they were instructed about earlier.

Now, upon taking hypnosis away, this recalled ability also vanished. This basically means that while synesthesia is innate to someone, when it's not being tapped, or when practice is not being done, the person might lose touch in time.

More on Synesthesia

Synesthia naturally means *together sensation*, and is considered a neurological phenomenon. When a person experiences synesthesia, cognitive and sensory pathways are stimulated in involuntary and automatic manners.

It's said that it's great because it makes a person more creative, and that's why it's best for a person to go through hypnosis every once in a while. If this doesn't happen, the person's ability to tap Synesthesia might degenerate, especially if he's in he's middle-aged already. Some consider it a gift; others, a treasure.

It is also best used when one is in a state of virtual reality, especially when it's used as treatment. Sensory distraction is improved because of this, as well as the improvement of one's attention span. What happens is that the way you perceive your environment gets twisted, so in turn, you tend to have a different way of seeing things, and you'd easily be immersed in the situation that you are in, without feeling tired or fragile about it.

Synesthesia may either be progressive (when people actually see, hear, and feel the projected colors, shapes, and the like), or associative (when people just have a strong connection between the stimulants and whatever it is that they trigger).

Cross-talk between various brain regions happen when Synesthesia is present. It is also said that when Synesthesia is induced by hypnosis, people who have sensory problems, insomnia, or who have suffered from stroke and head trauma, amongst others, would benefit a lot because the mechanism of their brain gets twisted the right way.

Interestingly enough, synesthesia is also pushed by ideasthesia—which is also tapped by hypnosis. Ideasthesia happens when stimulus is induced by the extraction of meaning, which means that the brain gets to understand things that it found hard to understand before.

The reason why synesthesia is easily tapped by hypnosis are as follows:

1. **Synesthesia works on one's memory**. Hypnosis could get back lost memories, and trigger the formation of new ones.

2. **Synesthesia is automatic and involuntary.** Again, when a person is under hypnosis, he doesn't really know what's happening to him, but then he submits to it because he feels that it's right—and it's naturally how the way things should go.

3. **Perceptions are extended.** This means that when one perceives something, a location is also triggered in his memory. For example, you may think about going to a certain place, or connecting a certain place to one of the memories you have.

4. **Synesthesia is simple**. It doesn't always have to deal with photographic memory, or about being good in memorization and all that. It just happens—and that's what's interesting about it.

5. **Synesthesia is affective.** Once you undergo Synesthesia, you'd be able to tap into your emotions, and would easily be able to interact with stimuli. Gestures and vocalizations are also indicators of affect.

There are various forms of Synesthesia, which are:

1. **Grapheme-Color Synesthesia**. This happens when numbers and alphabet are tinged with color, and commonalities are then seen between the letters. This also makes it easier for children to recognize and write letters. For example, R, is just P, with another slanted tail, or D is just B with a slash in the middle.

2. **Spatial Sequence.** In this form of Synesthesia, people see numerical points in space as numbers. To make it clearer, they tend to see number 1 as something near, 2 farther away, 3 even farther, and so on.

3. **Chromestesia.** There's also a condition called Chromestesia, where colors are associated with sounds. For example, when one hears a door being closed, a color is then triggered in his mind. Or, when he hears fireworks, he sees colors, too—and not just those that he sees in the sky. Sounds also change depending on the hues they see.

4. **Number Form.** Number Form is basically a "map" of numbers that one sees when he has numbers in his head.

5. **Ordinary Linguistic Personification.** This happens when ordered sequences are associated with personalities. This could either pertain to numbers, days, letters, months, and the like.

6. **Auditory-Tactile Synesthesia.** This happens when whatever people hear induces sensations in the body. It could either be present during birth, or could be prevalent in the latter stages of one's life. Not a lot of people experience this, though.

7. **Mirror Touch Synthesis.** This is kind of like Empathy, in such a way that the person experiencing it also feels the way that other people feel. A good example would be if some-

one accidentally steps on the foot of the person beside you, you'd also feel like someone stepped on you, too, even without actually being stepped on in the first place. According to medical experts, this mostly happens because of mirror neurons in one's brain—and that's why it could easily be tapped through hypnosis.

8. **Misophonia.** This is the kind of Synesthesia that you probably would not want to experience, unless you want to tap into the deepest parts of your soul. What happens here is that negative feelings are triggered by certain sounds you hear. However, it makes brain waves more connected to each other, which could provide you with clearer thinking in time.

9. **Lexical Gustatory Synesthesia.** Basically, this is the form of Synesthesia that describes how it's like to taste words upon hearing them. For example, when you hear the word bubbles, you think that it's sweet, even if it's not necessarily that way in real life.

Chapter 12

Hypnosis for Dermatology

Hypnodermatology is the term given to hypnosis when it's used to treat dermatologic infections.

Hypnosis could be used for dermatological procedures because it regulates blood flow, as well as other autonomic functions that one usually cannot control consciously. This is because there's a certain hypnotic relaxation response that happens when one undergoes hypnosis. Now, this response influences immune responses, especially when dealing with prick tests that are common for people with dermatological responses. Cellular responses are also affected by this.

Another reason why hypnosis works for dermatological problems is the fact that the mind could easily influence disease conditions, as well as physiologic responses. For example, when you feel itchy in a certain part of your body, and you tell yourself that you're fine, and it's not itchy enough, chances are you'd actually feel better because you would not focus on the fact that something is extremely itchy. This way, you also get to control destructive habits, such as scratching that may lead to pruritis or analgesia, and in turn would help you recover faster from your skin problems, as well as from surgery. In short, mind-body connection works better because of this.

Skin diseases with psychosomatic aspects are also easily dealt with because the skin becomes so responsive, especially when one has undergone hypnosis.

Why it works

If you're still wondering why hypnosis works in the treatment of skin problems, maybe you can put to mind the study done by the Harvard Medical Group.

As you well may know by now, skin is the body's largest organ, and that is why whatever the body goes through, the skin feels it first. It protects the body against injuries and modulates how the skin reacts to environmental influences, such as air pollution, heat and cold, and ultraviolet light.

There are certain cells in the body that can manufacture Vitamin D. Vitamin D is important for the skin as it keeps it looking radiant, and healthy. When a person is extremely stressed, these cells find it hard to make use of Vitamin D, which then results to greasy and unhealthy skin.

However, if one goes through hypnosis, he easily taps neuropeptides, also known as chemical messengers in the brain, to make sure that cells all do their jobs properly. This is because they could now differentiate stress from normal occurrences, and would no longer be wary of psychological substances that may alter the way the brain thinks.

Chronic Negative Stress has also been proven to worsen skin diseases and could disrupt the permeability of the skin. Loss of fluid could be prevented when one has gone through hypnosis because then, he would no longer be too stressed out.

Maybe, you should also begin to understand mind-skin conditions more to see how this all works out. Here are the three main categories you should think about:

1. **Psychophysiological**. These are conditions that happen physiologically but are triggered by emotional factors and stress. These may include acne, dermatitis, eczema, pruritis, hyperhidrosis, warts, and rosacea. Most, they could also be triggered by sweating, especially when one is in a stressful condition. Some of these may easily respond to topical medication, but when the conditions worsen, it's still best to let the person go through hypnosis already, just to alter the effects of the brain on the body.

2. **Primary Psychiatric.** These are skin disorders that are actually triggered by psychiatric factors. Examples include self-harm, chronic hair pulling, and even believing that the body has been infested by loads of organisms. This means that a person does not only have to go through dermatological evaluation, he also has to undergo psychiatric help, as well.

3. **Secondary Psychiatric.** Examples include psoriasis, acne, genital herpes, and vitiligo. They may socially stigmatize the skin, which means that when one suffers from these conditions, he'd also feel like he is being ridiculed by society, and that he does not want to be around people too much anymore. Some of them could even tend to be suicidal, or could resort to taking more medicine than necessary. With the help of Hypnosis, these people would be calmer, and would understand more about their conditions. They would take control, instead of letting their conditions take control of them!

How it works

To give you a better idea of how Hypnodermatology works for various kinds of skin problems, read on and find out!

Atopic Dermatitis. Basically, when you suffer from this, it means that your skin is chronically inflamed. Hypnosis works against Atopic Dermatitis because it controls stress levels, and helps promote relaxation. When this happens, skin stops chafing, and skin will easily be soothed. You'd also be glad to know that because of this, you'd also get an instant ego boost, and you would no longer feel the need to scratch. Even those who already use corticosteroid in the first place have stopped the usage by at least 60%!

Alopecia Areata. Alopecia also stands for spot baldness, or when one's hair suddenly falls off more frequently than usual.

What makes it worse is that sometimes, people have the tendency to keep on pulling their hair out even more. However, people who underwent hypnosis to control the way they react to Alopecia have been proven to get better, and have also experience hair regrowth.

Psoriasis. Psoriasis is known as a condition where scaly, red areas are produced on one's skin. Psoriasis is often caused by stress, more than external elements. At least 75% of people who underwent hypnosis to cure Psoriasis have shown improvement, especially when the sensory imagery projectile is used. Research also has it that Psoriasis could be used as adjunct therapy for resistant psoriasis, too!

Furuncles. Furuncles are often caused by boils that then inflame the hair follicles. Even those who have been suffering from furuncles for a long time could still benefit from hypnosis. Case in point, there was this man who started having furuncles when he was just 16. He's in his 30s now, and then he underwent hypnosis, and in a matter of five weeks, he already saw vast improvements. He said that not only did hypnosis treat the disease, it helped sustain his mental well-being, too, and have lessened his need for taking antibiotics. Susceptibility to recurring infection is also prevented because of hypnosis.

Veruca Vulgaris. Veruca Vulgaris also stands for warts, and it has been proven that at least 53% of people who have it, and who underwent hypnosis have shown improvement in their conditions.

Urticaria. Another term for Urticaria is Warts, and hypnosis works great against this condition, especially if the patient is still in his pre-teens. Those who underwent hypnosis have said that they felt extremely relaxed, and they felt like they would be able to deal with their condition better. In the case of 15 participants, at least 8 have shown improvement, and have ultimately gotten better over time. Over-all, at least 80% of people who have hives could benefit greatly from hypnosis.

Venipuncture. Venipuncture is the act of getting intravenous access for venuos blood sampling, and is usually used on children to help determine the condition they're in. Children who were put on hypnosis have said that they felt less anxious in having to deal with treatment, and in the process of getting their blood taken, compared to those who only went through Venipuncture alone.

Here is a sample script for psoriasis sufferers.

You are here because you have made a decision to take control. You have decided to allow yourself to be at your best health. You are now ready to put psoriasis away and leave it in the past. You are letting the condition go. It is now just an unwanted memory.

From this moment forward, you choose to be healthy. You decide to have healthy skin, and you are in complete control. You now realize that you are in control of your health. You get what you desire. Your subconscious is strong enough to attract health. You desire healthy skin and you receive healthy skin. Your subconscious, with the strength of your desire, allows your body to grow healthy skin.

I wonder if you can imagine your skin growing. Can you feel it? The power comes from your subconscious fueled by your strong desire. Every single cell in your body is working towards a common goal. They are working together to grow this healthy and beautiful skin. Slowly and slowly, healthy skin grows... You now have the skin that you desire the most. You now have the skin you always wanted. Everything feels real. This beautiful and healthy skin is real. You made it happen because you allowed your mind to let this healthy skin grow. You did it. This is your choice.

This is your choice because you are in control of your desires. You are in control of your body, of your health. You feel completely relaxed, calm and at ease. You are comfortable in your healthy skin.

Chapter 13

Hypnosis and IVF Treatment

People who have fertility problems, and who are undergoing IVF can also benefit from hypnosis, apparently.

A study done by members of the Soroka University in Israel showed that at least 28% of women who underwent hypnotism actually have gotten pregnant, as compared to 14% who were not hypnotized.

According to this study, the transplant of eggs through IVF becomes easier because when a woman is hypnotized, her uterus contracts, making it easier for eggs to pass through, and make their home inside.

Women who undergo IVF could also be stressed, especially because of their situation. This is the reason why sometimes, the procedure does not really produce viable results. But, when one goes through hypnotism, her body begins to understand that she is okay. Her mind calms her down; her body is soothed. This way, the process becomes more natural and her body begins to understand that those eggs are now part of her.

How it happens

Interestingly, when you go through hypnotherapy for IVP, your situation will be assessed, and a perfect plan will be created for you. It happens this way.

1. **Outcome**. Wait, what? Outcome first? No, it's not what you think. What happens here is that when you ask to go through hypnotherapy for IVF, the therapist asks you what you want out of it. What is the outcome that you have in mind? In order to be emotionally prepared for the therapy, you do have to know and understand what you want. For example:

    a. You want to have a baby.

    b. You want to feel the child in your tummy.

    c. You want to be a mother.

    d. You want to experience both pleasure and pain of being a mother.

You have to be extremely detailed in saying what you want the outcome to be. It all starts from there.

2. **Balance.** Now, the therapist would formulate a plan on how to restore balance in your life. You have to keep in mind that even if a lot of people want to try IVF, they all have various reasons, and different lifestyles to keep. So, it would be impossible to say that a certain plan would work for everyone,

and also, it would be impossible for you to plan it yourself, too.

It is imperative that in creating balance, changes have to be made. These changes have something to do with hobbies, lifestyle, relationships, and the like. One would be put through hypnosis to possibly retrieve some lost memories and see how one's upbringing, or wellbeing in the past could work alongside who she is now.

Also, through hypnosis, one would be taught how to focus on the better things in life—or on things that make her happy so that she would not be too stressed out and could expect the procedure to work. This way, you would be able to exert more energy in taking care of yourself and your baby, instead of focusing on the negative things in life.

Another change would be, if you are too busy, you of course have to try to cut yourself some slack. You have to give up on some things, because really, you cannot have everything all at the same time.

Upon hearing these things during hypnosis, one would wake up with a clearer mind, and with the motivation to do better, and be better in life, instead of just letting things as they come. You would no longer be like a leaf in the wind, but rather a person who has goals, and who has the ability to let those goals come to life.

3. **Resolve.** In this stage, you get ready to face your fears, and understand how you can move past them. You would also be able to tap into your deepest worries, and worst fears.

For example, oftentimes, people who want to go through IVF are those who have long been disappointed because they could not have a baby. They're the ones who feel ashamed of themselves because they feel like they have ruined their chances of getting a real family, and that they have disappointed their family and relatives, and themselves, too.

All these things can make one feel incompetent, and can make one feel like her whole life, and the meaning of her life would only be complete because of a child.

Under hypnosis, one would be able to say how she truly feels. Because sometimes, the need for a baby does not mean that it's the only thing that can make you happy; or that you would not be complete without a baby. Rather, having a baby is about just the experience, and the joy of being a parent—but that you can still be fine with or without it.

Hence, by the end of resolve, you'd be able to understand yourself better, and know why you actually want a baby. In short, you would no longer feel like you should have a baby just so you could fit in society, but would understand what makes it important for you. It would help you get in that serene state, and make you feel so much better about yourself.

4 **Enhance and Prepare.** During this stage of hypnosis, one would be shown images or graphs that have something to do with IVF, being pregnant, and being a parent, in general.

A perfect example would be a therapist giving you a CD or manual that contains information about IVF: from stimulation, to the transfer of embryo, to implantation. Of course, when you get to see or read this, you'd be able to put your mind to a state of readiness. You would be able to tell yourself that you are actually going to go through IVF, and that it could work for you.

Also, it helps you understand that treatment is going to happen soon. You can think of it as research materials that you use when you're in a class, or when you have lessons to learn.

Being prepared for the treatment would mean you'd be anchored to do whatever you can to make things work for you. You would no longer feel alone, and rather, would see yourself as someone who's capable of making her dreams come true!

5. **Support.** And finally, during this stage, you would feel that you have all the support you need, and that you're capable of making IVF work for you, and of having a baby at the end of the process.

You'd also be ready not only for IVF, but also for the experience of being a parent.

Successes of using hypnosis for IVF are high. You'd also be surprised to know that some of those who underwent this procedure actually not only responded to IVF, but some of them have gotten pregnant in the natural course.

Not only that, they were also able to keep themselves at peace, and help themselves throughout the pregnancy, making the process easier for them, and helping them deliver healthy babies, while making sure that their health as mothers did not and would not suffer.

Chapter 14 - Hypnosis for IBS

Yes, Hypnosis can also actually work for IBS (Irritable Bowel Syndrome)!

IBS affects around 15% of the population at any given time, and research has it that 71% of people who suffer from IBS have responded well to hypnosis!

Now, how exactly does one know that he's suffering from IBS? Well, you can take a look at the symptoms below:

1. **Abdominal pain.** Of course, when your stomach is hurting, chances are there is something wrong inside!
2. **Constipation.** This is never a good thing.
3. **Diarrhea.** Diarrhea is actually considered as one of the most common symptoms of IBS. It can definitely make anyone feel uncomfortable and unproductive.
4. **Rushing to bowel.**
5. **Vomiting, belching, and nausea.** This happens possibly because of gasses, and also the acids in your system.
6. **A feeling of incomplete emptying of bowels.**
7. **Bloated stomach.**

People who suffer from IBS and want to go through hypnosis will be asked about their symptoms, and about how they really feel inside to assess the gravity of the situation. Levels of anxiety and depression are also tested, because these are some of the side effects of IBS, too.

According to at least 70% of patients who underwent hypnosis, their IBS has alleviated, and the severities of effects were lessened, too. This is essentially true for most female patients, who are also part of the majority who suffer from IBS.

Why it works

Hypnosis works for people who have IBS mainly because:

1. Individuals who have already undergone other IBS healing methods would be set in a state of healing, even if those methods have not worked for them at first try. These methods include:

    a. Taking Alosetrone and Lubiprostene.

    b. Taking Xifaxan and Linaclotide.

    c. Taking Eluxadoline.

2. The healing powers of the mind are utilized, and when this happens, you're able to tell yourself that you will get better, and that you'll be able to fight IBS, even if it seems hard at first.

3. There are no side effects, unlike when taking medication for the said condition.

4. It's generally enjoyable and relaxing, which is important because this is the kind of medical condition that could take a toll on anyone.

5. Other symptoms, and medical conditions, such as tension headaches and migraine are treated, as well.

6. The effects are long-term. Just because one isn't in hypnosis anymore does not mean that he would no longer reap the rewards of going through it in the first place.

And it works better when...

According to professional hypnotists, the procedure works better in the treatment of IBS when:

1. Products that contain carageenan are eliminated in one's diet;

2. At least 500 to 1000mg of turmeric is taken once a day;

3. One intakes slippery elm powder, which could be mixed with boiling water, sugar, and cinnamon;

4. Peppermint oil is taken, and;

5. Probiotics are also taken.

One can also try:

1. **Biofeedback.** Biofeedback is a machine that helps the mind and body to make use of neurons that pertain to healing. This then controls muscle tension, heart rate, blood pressure, and brainwave frequency. Sensitivity and precision of the body are also improved because of this.

2. **Relaxing Breath Techniques.** As the name suggests, these breathing exercises are meant to make you feel relaxed, and help bring you to that state of peace that will make IBS healing easier. Try the ones listed below.

Relaxing Breath Techniques

1. **Bellows Breath.** This is a yogic breathing technique that increases alertness and promotes vital energy. Here's how you should do it:

    a. Use your nose to rapidly inhale and exhale, and make sure to relax and keep your mouth closed while doing so. Make sure that your breaths are in the same direction, and that they're equal.

    b. For starters, try three in and out breaths also for a matter of 3 seconds each. Make sure that you use the diaphragm to breathe, and that you breathe normally after each cycle.

    c. Also, remember not to do more than 15 breaths for your first try because it might be too taxing.

1. **Breath Counting.** As the name suggests, it's all about counting your breaths, and is pretty much a zen exercise. Here's how you should do it:

a. Sit straight while in a comfortable position.

b. Incline your head forward and close your eyes while taking deep breath. Just let your breathing flow naturally, and don't overdo it.

c. Count one as you exhale. You don't have to say it out loud, but do tell it to yourself.

d. Then, next breath, count two, three for the next, and so on.

e. To start a new cycle, just start from one again until you find time to exhale.

2. **4-7-8 or Relaxing Breath Technique.** It's said that this is one of the easiest exercises to do, and that it requires almost no effort. It kind of looks complicated in the beginning, but it gets easier once you get the hang of it. Check it out below:

a. Sit straight and then place the tip of your tongue, and make sure that it stays there throughout the rest of the exercise. If it makes you feel uncomfortable, you could just choose to purse your lips while doing so.

b. Use your mouth to completely exhale. This means that a "wooosh" sound must be heard when you exhale.

c. Inhale quietly through your nose as you close your mouth, and then go and count to 4.

d. For seven counts, hold your breath.

e. Again, use your mouth to exhale completely. Remember that the woosh sound has to be heard.

f. Inhale once more.

g. Repeat the process for 3 to 4 times more.

Also, when looking for an IBS Hypnotist, make sure that you look for someone who is...

1. **A professional.** One could be a professional hypnotist, but if he doesn't know how to work his way around IBS, you might be in trouble. Choose someone who knows something about the said condition.

2. **One who has experience in Clinical Hypnosis.** He has to have significant experience in this so you could be sure that he knows what he's doing.

3. **Knows IBS protocols.** Again, refer to rule number 1. It's kind of a sensitive condition so you have to make sure that the person is experienced enough and that he really knows what he's doing.

Use the sample script below as reference to create your own script. Read and record the script so you can self-hypnotize yourself out of IBS or help someone you know suffering from the same condition.

I wonder if you could imagine a glass, a clear glass, any kind of glass of any shape... That's it... You can see it now...

Imagine the glass being slowly filled up with a liquid substance... It is not just any liquid substance. It is special... This special liquid substance can prevent anything from hurting and irritating your stomach... Slowly, the glass is filled with this special liquid substance that prevents stomach irritation...

Now imagine a hand reaching out, taking hold of the glass filled with special liquid substance. Look, it is your own hand... Visualize holding the glass and raising it to your mouth... That's it... Closer and closer... Visualize yourself drinking the special liquid substance that prevents stomach irritation... You are now drinking... You can now feel the special liquid substance flowing down your stomach... You feel the warmth... You feel relaxed as it the special liquid substance travels through your body...

Imagine the special liquid substance wrapping around your stomach... Could you imagine how it feels? It feels good... Your stomach feels great... The special liquid is now protecting your stomach. Your stomach is now shielded against irritation. Your stomach is protected... You feel comfortable. You feel safe... Nothing bothers you now...

Chapter 15

Hypnosis against Phobias

Everyone has phobias, and of course, phobias really are not rational. While some phobias may have been caused by traumatic experiences, others are just there for no reason at all.

Sometimes, people don't really mind having phobias, but there are times when their phobias could make them feel like they couldn't do so much in life—and that's when it hurts the most.

There are various kinds of phobias. Examples include:

1. **Animal Phobias.** Of course, this has something to do with fearing certain animals, mostly snakes, dogs, frogs, spiders, and the like.

2. **Injury/Blood Injection Phobias.** This has something to do with fear of medical practices, such as being injected, being in hospitals, seeing blood, and having to deal with injuries.

3. **Natural Environment Phobias.** Examples include the fear of heights, darkness, water, storms, lightning, etc.

4. **Situational Phobias.** This happens when someone expe-

riences things that he actually does not want to be in. For example, the fear of falling is tapped when one walks through a bridge or on stairs with gaps in them. Other examples include driving, passing through tunnels, being around other people, dating, etc.

It is said that phobias are often the result of "mis-wiring" in the brain. When one undergoes hypnosis, the parts of his brain that have something to do with phobias. One would develop better control, too.

How it works

Under hypnosis, you will be brought towards a calm state of mind, so in turn, your brainwaves would slow down, and you could then engage your subconscious mind.

It is also said that simple daydreaming is already a good example of hypnosis, especially if you can't remember a few minutes in your day while you're in the said state. This way, the subconscious mind could be desensitized and change could then easily be created.

Another good thing that could work is NLP or Neuro-Linguistic Programming. This way, the brain gets to access the triggers of one's worries, and in turn, the person would be able to understand the root of the problem, and in turn heal the phobia. In short, the feelings of anxiety or fear are replaced by feelings of being in control and being calm.

When you learn how to let go of your phobias, you also learn to develop a better sense of being. You get to be a more confident individual because you know that you have nothing to fear, and that you're ready to face the world and whatever challenges or situations it'll bring.

Yes, you can live with your phobias. That is true. However, it would be so much better if you can live life in a way that you would no longer be limited by your fears, right? And that's why it would be best for you to undergo hypnosis!

To help you get started with creating your own scripts for addressing phobias, here's a sample script targeted to address arachnophobia.

Addressing Fear of Spiders

I would like you to think about a memory, a happy memory, a wonderful one, a memory that makes you feel safe... Imagine it clearly in your head... That's it... I want you to nod your head as soon as you have a clear picture of this happy memory, this wonderful memory, this memory that makes you feel safe... That's it...

From this moment forward, when you think about spiders, I want you to focus on this happy and wonderful memory, this memory that makes you feel safe. I want you to picture it clearly in your mind, this happy scene... So when you think of spiders from this moment on, you associate it with this happy scene, this wonderful and safe memory... Then slowly, release the thought. Let it go like something unimportant... You can do this... The past is in the past. It is just a memory... You can let it fade away, float away, farther and farther it goes, safer and safer you feel... Ready... Let it go now.

Chapter 16

Hypnosis for Self-Esteem

Another issue that most people face is having low self-esteem, and yes, it can be treated with the help of hypnosis, too!

Basically, self-esteem is having belief in yourself, and knowing that you are capable, and that you deserve great things in your life. It means having respect for yourself, and treating yourself the best way you can.

When one has low self-esteem, he kind of tends to sabotage himself in such a way that he no longer feels the need to put himself out there; to be part of the world in a certain way. Having low self-esteem may also mean that one would suffer from anxiety, and from being consumed by pain and self-hate. They do not realize that they're capable of doing great things, too!

How to know if one has low self-esteem

Here the things that you have to be aware of. If you can relate to any of these, it may mean that you're suffering from low self-esteem.

1. Withdrawing from your peers, or any form of social contact.

2. Self-medication. This only does not have to do with taking drugs (whether intermittent or prohibited), but also food, drinks, shopping, and gambling. Sometimes, you tend to be addicted to something because you have no idea how to deal with yourself anymore.

3. Suffering from too much nerves, anxiety, and panic attacks that can be triggered by even the littlest thing.

4. Giving up on your goals. Sometimes, you'd feel like there's no more light at the end of the tunnel, and you're no longer motivated to achieve your goals.

5. Procrastination. This happens when you push things off for later even if you know you can do them now.

6. Not being satisfied with your appearance, and being ultimately insecure.

7. Self-harming/Self-mutilation.

8. Negative self-talk, or telling yourself you're not good enough and you deserve every bad thing that happens to you.

9. Comparing yourself to others and thinking everyone's better than you.

10. Putting yourself down, especially when others are around.

Of course, when these are around, you can expect that...

1. You might suffer from physical pain.
2. You'd have extremely poor self-image that may make you feel like you should just hide from society, and you cannot be the person you want to be.
3. You'd lose or gain too much weight.
4. You'd be depressed, and have a lot of suicidal thoughts.
5. You'd lose function, and sexual desire.
6. You would have lots of harmful addictions.
7. Your career might suffer and be stagnant, or you might also lose your job.
8. You'd have financial problems.
9. Your personal relationships would be damaged.
10. And, you would ultimately have difficulty in achieving your goals.

How Hypnosis Works

1. **Some of the hypnosis tools and techniques that will be used to improve self-esteem include:**
    a. Progressive Relaxation
    b. Deep Focused Breathing (using the diaphragm)

c. Self-esteem visualization

d. Inner Childwork

e. Interactive Self-Esteem Building

f. Negative Self Talk Redirection

g. Positive Trigger Association

h. Negative Trigger Desensitization

i. Resource State Creation

j. Positive Memory Revival

2. **Low-self esteem components would be identified.** Again, you have to remember that it's always essential to understand the root of the problem, including its triggers, issues, symptoms, history, etc.

3. **Goals will be set.** You will have to tell your therapist what it is that you want to happen in your life, and why exactly you want them to happen.

4. **Self-esteem hypnosis will then be done.**

5. **Progress will of course, be tracked.**

6. **New goals would also be set so that the progress would not be stagnant and you wouldn't feel lost or contrived to just doing a single thing.**

7. **Strategies would also be revised.** Just like everything in life, it's important to set new strategies, depending on what you now want to happen in your life.

8. **Steps will be repeated as necessary**. The number of sessions you have to go through would be based upon your progress.

Chapter 17

Hypnosis for Smokers

You've learned that hypnosis can be effective in treating various conditions including bad habits such as smoking. Every year, there are 5 million deaths caused by the ill effects of cigarette smoking. Cigarettes do not kill smokers instantly. Rather, cigarette smoking kills slowly and painfully. Its effects vary from affecting a person's sex drive to incapacitating both the body and the brain.

We are all familiar with the deadly effects of this bad habit so why are there people who stick to it? Isn't the human brain built for self-preservation? Why then would people willingly throw away their lives for a puff? The reasons vary. Some people smoke because they feel a sense of relief in it. Others feel pleasure. One thing is for sure. Smoking is addictive. Cigarette smoking must be treated for what it is. It is an addiction.

How does addiction work?

In order to treat smoking or any kind of addiction appropriately, you must understand how it works first. Addiction twists the brain's chemical reward mechanism. The same mechanism is responsible for making us feel pleasure when we learn things.

In which case, the reward mechanism is not bad, but it can be negatively affected by an addiction.

Addiction starts in a simple way. Do you notice how excited you feel about something because you know it will make you feel good? Our attention is focused on the anticipation and it somehow puts us in an addictive trance. Behind this excitement is a brain chemical called dopamine. It works like a natural cocaine. After we've done or had that something we were so excited about, we then feel a sense of satisfaction. Behind this warm feeling of satisfaction is another brain chemical called endorphins.

These brain chemicals exist primarily to encourage humans to learn and master skills. They are important for survival. We would not eat or drink if not for them. We would not consume food and water if we don't feel internally rewarded. Essentially, this internal reward mechanism is built for survival and yet it can be twisted by certain behaviors that threat our very survival like smoking.

Another important aspect of addiction you need to understand is habituation. Because there is pleasure in doing something, we continue to do it. Just like when you learn to play a musical instrument for instance, when you learn to play a tune for the first time, you feel a great feeling of satisfaction so you try to learn another and you feel satisfied again. You become excited to learn playing a new tune and the first tune you learned becomes second nature.

It now feels easier so the reward from playing it is diminished. The same is true for addiction. Tolerance builds up so you feel like your body needs more to get the same sense of satisfaction you felt the first time. Addicts chase after that buzz.

People fall into an addiction because their internal reward mechanism is messed up. Human nature dictates that when something is rewarding, we are bound to chase after it. We are bound to repeat the same behavior over and over to feel satisfaction.

How does hypnosis work for smoking?

Hypnosis will not work unless the person is willing to quit smoking in the first place. Understand the situation from the smoker's perspective. Ultimately, this person feels torn. One part of him wants to stop, the other wants to continue. The goal of hypnosis is to strengthen that part of him that wants to stop the habit so the other takes the backseat. And there are several ways to do this.

How do most people convince their smoker friends to quit and why their attempts don't work? They usually point out the ill effects of smoking. They tell their smoker friends that soon, their arteries will rot and they will suffer impotence, or that their eyesight will suffer, their gums will soften and lungs will be impaired. It does not work because smokers already know these facts. Of course, they don't want to suffer but their need for satisfaction feels much more urgent than their health.

After all, they don't suffer immediately after each puff. They don't feel the consequences right now so they are more focused on the feeling of pleasure. They know the ill effects of smoking in theory but it does not feel real at the moment.

So how do you convince someone to quit smoking? There is no single approach to this. It may work for one but not to another but it mostly does. What is this approach I am talking about? Appeal to their beliefs.

The multi-billion tobacco industry exists and thrives because of people who are willing serve and support the "cause." What is the cause of the rich tobacco industry? There is only one cause. It certainly isn't to better people lives. The single cause is to make profits. In other words, smokers lay down their health, their money and their lives for this cause. Is it a cause worth losing one's life for?

Hypnosis works in helping people quit smoking this way. Through hypnosis, you or someone you know can grow out of the habit. This is possible by correcting the internal reward mechanism.

The circumstances vary from one individual to another. You can start by asking yourself or someone you know these questions.

1. How long have you been into smoking?

2. What's your reason for starting?

3. Did or does someone in your life smoke? Is it a person you look up to? Who is it?

4. Have you ever made attempts to stop? What kind of methods did you try to quit? Why were these attempts unsuccessful?

5. How much do you smoke a day? How much does it cost you?

6. If you can save this money by quitting, how will you be able to use it or what will you use it for?

7. What are your top reasons for wanting to quit?

8. Are you afraid of quitting? What are your hesitations?

9. Are there people in your life who will appreciate it if you quit? Who are they? Are they important to you?

10. Are you aware that smoking is dangerous to your health? Do you believe that it is?

11. Have you ever experienced coughing or shortness of breath? Do you experience other health problems because of this habit?

12. Why do you enjoy smoking and when do you enjoy it the most? Do you find it most enjoyable in the morning, with coffee or as a reward?

13. Are your breaks spent on smoking?

14. Do you smoke in the car/ vehicle?

15. Do you have a tendency to get up in the middle of the night to smoke?

16. Do you smoke when you are on the phone?

17. Does smoking make you feel certain or confident about yourself?

18. Do you smoke more when you overeat or upset or bored?

19. Do you believe that smoking helps you?

20. Are you ready to quit?

The answers to these questions can help you unlock the inner motivations for smoking. The insights you gain are useful in coming up with powerful suggestions so you can quit smoking or help someone you know stop the habit.

Smokers aren't alike in their motivations. For hypnosis to work for smoking cessation, you have to figure out the specific motivations that drive you or someone you know to smoke. After the progressive muscle relaxation, you can use the general sample script below in preparation for the therapeutic suggestions.

Now, I want you to let your unconscious mind picture yourself standing at the top of a flight of stairs, wide and brightly lit. In a few moments, I will ask you to start walking down the stairs. I will count from 10 to 1. As I countdown and guide you through the stairs, you will feel more and more deeply relaxed and comfortable about leaving smoking behind. You will feel more able to enjoy your life without cigarettes. You will be more able to look forward to a life without smoking. I want to remind you that you can take your time in going down the stairs. Walk at your own pace because you are in control of your smoking habit.

Ready. We start at 10... You are relaxed and comfortable. 9... Deeper and deeper... 8.... Take your time to enjoy this experience of light trance state as you go deeper and deeper. 7... In this state, it is easier for your unconscious mind to work. 6... Your unconscious mind knows you best. 5... Take all the suggestions and become more open to becoming a non-smoker. 4... Believe that you can enjoy life without cigarettes. 3... It may surprise you how good it feels to be smoke-free... 2... 1... Look forward to your life without cigarettes. Now, imagine yourself standing at the foot of the stairs...

Keep listening to the sound of my voice. Allow me to address your unconscious mind about an important matter, a matter that is of extreme importance to you. You are here now because you want to quit smoking and you will...

General Suggestions

Whenever you find yourself in a place, situation or mood where you would have smoked in the past, you will feel confident, relaxed and pleased because you have no desire to light a cigarette. You feel positive. You feel better and very much in control. You are in complete control of your actions, your feelings, your thoughts. As the days pass by, you become and continue to become someone who has left smoking behind. Keep this in mind. You are responsible for this. You are in control. You did this. You can be pleased and proud of yourself for breaking free...

Addressing Mood as Trigger for Smoking

Notice that you have a strong resolve to break your smoking habit. You are taking control. You will now feel that the moods that affected you in the past, the moods that have tempted you to reach out for a smoke are fading... You are in control now. You are relaxed and becoming more relaxed in all situations. You feel more confident, happy and proud that you no longer smoke...

Addressing Situations that Trigger the Habit

You are aware of the situations, the situations that have affected you in certain ways, in ways that you would have smoked. Now that you are more aware, you can proudly say, "I am in complete control. I am not lighting a cigarette. I can do it without smoking..." You will immediately feel your strength, a sense of being in control of all these situations...

Addressing Excuses

You have decided to become a non-smoker. You have made a decision to be someone who has left smoking in the past... From this moment forward, you will see to it that you never, under any circumstances smoke again. When someone offers you a stick, remember how good it feels to become a non-smoker. That part of you is a thing of the past. You have stopped. You have quit. You have broken free. Now, you feel proud to say, "I am a non-smoker." Saying these words reinforces your resolve. You feel truly in control, in control of your habits and other things. No matter what happens, you have control...

Chapter 18

Hypnosis for Sleeping Better

Good quality sleep does wonders to a person's mood, disposition and performance. Someone who sleeps better is likely to feel healthier and happier. That's because sleep allows us to nourish our bodily systems. It helps strengthen our immunity, our lungs, heart and skin health. Everything is simply better when you sleep well.

Naturally, a poor sleeping pattern is bad news. It makes someone irritable. It affects performance. Poor sleep can lead to various health ailments as well. It makes a person more prone to stress and other health issues.

Now there certainly are various ways to ensure that you are getting a good night's rest. You can make sure that your bedroom is the ideal sleeping environment. Soft and comfortable bed and pillows; fresh sheets and blankets; quiet, dimly lit, clutter-free and cool: these are the main qualities of a good sleeping environment and you have to make sure that your bedroom is up to these standards.

Sometimes, improving the environment is enough. In some cases, however, the cause of poor sleep are poor habits. It is important to set up consistent sleep and wake times. You also need to limit brain stimulation at least an hour before you hit the sack. You need to have a ritual to prepare you to bed. You must slowly wind down. Avoid night caps at least 3 hours before you retire. Have your meals 2 to 3 hours before your sleep schedule. Put away your computer, phone and other gadgets so you can sleep peacefully.

What happens then if none of these things work? Can hypnosis help you?

How it works?

You have probably heard of the counting sheep technique. It is a type of self hypnosis that induces sleep. In order to fall asleep, the first thing that happens is that your mental focus makes a switch from external to internal reality. When the mind makes the switch, images start to be generated. They come from a specific part of your brain, the same area that is responsible for imagination and dreams.

With this said, sleep can be induced by assisting your brain to make the switch from external to internal reality by imagining things that encourage it. Use your imagination for things that make you feel good. Never use it for worrying. That will only cause your body to produce stress hormones. These hormones make you more alert. It defeats the purpose of inducing sleep.

Because of its ability to make a person feel relaxed and put the conscious mind at the backseat, hypnosis is a beneficial tool that you can use to help people who have trouble sleeping. It does not even have to be limited to counting sheep. There are in fact, several techniques that can be used. For instance, you can use a guided journey to relaxation. Imagine walking on a beautiful beach with the light breeze touching your skin, the feel of the sand on your feet.

You can take a relaxing walk in a marvelous garden with flowers of different colors and fragrance bloom, where you can hear the birds singing and the sound of leaves as they are swayed by the wind. The key is you have to put yourself in a pleasant place. Imagine the sensations in your mind. When you begin to enjoy the feeling of calmness, embrace relaxation. You can then enter internal reality and begin a beautiful restful sleep.

Color Visualization

This technique features envisioning the color spectrum. The progression starts with red, orange, yellow, green, blue and ends with violet. When you reach the last color in the spectrum, you become ready to take a deep and healthy sleep. After induction to hypnosis and deepening the relaxation state, you can then proceed with your eyes still closed and visualize colors.

Visualize the first color, red. Think about things in this color like the flesh of a watermelon or the petals of a red rose, a red blanket, a red car... Think about anything in red. Hold on to the thought for a few moments and when you're ready, you can say, "I am now moving to orange. When I reach violet, I will be ready to take a deep and healthy sleep."

Visualize the second color, orange. What are orange things you can think of aside from the fruit? Think about a pumpkin, the inside of mango, an orange shirt or orange paint. Hold it in. take your time and when you're ready, say this "I am now moving to yellow. When I reach violet, I will be ready to take a deep and healthy sleep."

Visualize the third color, yellow. What images come to your mind when you think yellow? Think banana and lemon. Again, hold it in. Then you can tell yourself this "I am now moving to green. When I reach violet, I will be ready to take a deep and healthy sleep."

Visualize the fourth color, green. Picture green pastures, a forest, fresh green leaves, grass, spinach or lettuce. When you are ready, say this "I am now moving to blue. When I reach violet, I will be ready to take a deep and healthy sleep."

Visualize the fifth color, blue. Think of objects that can help make it easier for you to imagine this color like the color of the sky, a swimming pool or the ocean. Take your time and move on when you're ready, say "I am now moving to violet. The moment I see violet, I will fall into a deep and healthy sleep."

Visualize violet. Stay on this. Keep seeing violet until you fall asleep...

Alternatively, you can record your voice reading this sample script or read it to someone you want to help who's having trouble sleeping too.

Close your eyes and relax. Notice how tension is released from your body at each breath, from the top of your head, easing your facial muscles to your nape and neck. As you continue to breathe slowly, feel the way it eases your shoulders and jaw down to your arms and fingers. Now the calming energy travels from your chest to your abdomen, from your pelvic area down to your legs, feet and toes. You are no completely relaxed. You are free. That's it...

Take a deep breath and hold it for a few seconds. Slowly release your breath and relax more. Take another, deeper, hold it in and now let go... Allow the tension to leave you as you slowly release your breath. Breathe in deeply and as you do imagine that positive energy is entering your body... slowly exhale. Relax and feel peace...

Now, think about sleeping. Remember this feeling of relaxation, of calmness, of peace. I want you to remember how this feels like when you retire to your bed at night. Every time you go to bed, you will feel as relaxed as you are at this moment, so relaxed that you are ready to welcome sleep. The thoughts, the worries that usually bother you will now go away. They would fly, float in the wind and leave.

You are able to relax every nerve and muscle in your body, your mind is at peace. You feel comfortable. Everything feels soft and comfortable like you are being wrapped up in a soft, warm blanket. As you relax more, you feel much more at ease. If you could go deeper, you feel much better. If you could feel better, you go much deeper. That's right...

Sleep takes over. You feel like you are floating in the air, lying on soft clouds. You are lulled to sleep. Now you are able to see yourself. You are fully rested. You are ready to face everything in store for the day because you are fully rested, your energy restored, you are able to think clearly, you are positive...

From this moment forward, when you find yourself restless in bed at night, all you need to say is "relax." When you say the word "relax," you will immediately feel peaceful and relaxed. Say it quietly with your mind, "relax..." You welcome deep and healthy sleep. Say it again, "relax." This word will remind you of how comfortable, safe, relaxed and at peace you are at this moment. When you say this word, "relax," your desire to rest your eyes becomes stronger. "Relax..."

From now on, you will sleep better. You will sleep safe and sound... "Relax..." You will wake up every morning with a smile on your face because you feel refreshed and completely relaxed...

That's it... Now on the count of three, you can drift back to the present. Slowly open your eyes. You feel nicer, calmer and more positive. Open your eyes with a smile. Allow the positive energy to come out from within you. One... Two... Three...

Chapter 19 - Hypnosis for Success

In achieving and maximizing success, attitude plays a huge role. Attitude is related to focus, so when you have a strong attitude for success, you have a strong focus. A laser focused mind is in a hypnotic trance. It is not just about focusing, though. It is equally important to carefully choose the content of focus.

Do you expect to accomplish anything with a negative attitude? No. When you are negative, you become overwhelmed with doubts. Negativity is not only an unpleasant feeling. It also make things more difficult. If you have a negative attitude, you always expect things to go wrong. You expect failure intentionally or unintentionally.

What a huge difference a positive attitude makes! A positive attitude can make an otherwise difficult situation more doable. A person with a positive attitude seeks solutions while a negative person focuses only on the problems and the difficulty of the tasks. While a negative person attracts failure, a positive person always expects success.

Where do attitudes come from?

Attitudes are learned and they are learned in two ways. For one, you may condition yourself to a certain attitude. Two, you may be conditioned into a certain attitude by people around you. This conditioning is a hypnotic experience. That's right. Hypnosis can happen while you are conscious, wide awake and it may also last for only a few seconds. Attitudes like negativity, anger, addiction, depression and anxiety are hypnotic trance states.

How is this possible? Do you remember what we said about focus earlier? When you are focused, you are in a hypnotic trance. These negative emotions occur because you narrowly focus on this negativity. Then you combine focus with imagination. It is a complete recipe for hypnosis. Now imagine what difference you can make when you use your focus and imagination on positive things.

How does hypnosis help for creating success?

Hypnosis can either influence success or failure. Hypnosis creates expectations. These expectations become embedded in your personality. They become your instinct. Instinct works automatically. When you allow yourself to be conditioned into negative attitude, everything else in your life follows.

On the other hand, when hypnosis is used appropriately to condition yourself into positivity, it reflects in your actions and decisions. Positive thinking is not about creating unrealistic expectations. It is simply a change of perspective. When you worry about something that has not happened yet, is it realistic? It isn't.

Positive thinking is about assessing the situation objectively. Rather than focusing on things you have no control of, you can begin to realize the importance of focusing on things you can actually control like how you respond to challenging situations. When you do this, you become more capable to solve problems. You become more productive because you become more capable of handling matters.

After progressive relaxation and deepening techniques, you can proceed with the following scripts or you can refer to them to create your own script for success.

For Abundance

Close your eyes and relax. Notice how tension is released from your body at each breath, from the top of your head, easing your facial muscles to your nape and neck. As you continue to breathe slowly, feel the way it eases your shoulders and jaw down to your arms and fingers. Now the calming energy travels from your chest to your abdomen, from your pelvic area down to your legs, feet and toes. You are no completely relaxed. You are free. That's it...

In a few moments, I would like you to take three deep breaths. As you breathe in, imagine reaching out and welcoming abundance and prosperity in your life. And as you breathe out, imagine releasing the belief of lack and scarcity. As you breathe deeply and exhale slowly, you feel more positive, more blessed, more prosperous and abundant. Ready... Now, take a deep breath and hold it for a few seconds. Slowly release your breath and relax more. Take another, deeper, hold it in, you are welcoming prosperity and abundance in your life and now slowly exhale... Let the belief of scarcity leave you. Breathe in deeply and as you do imagine that positive energy is entering your body... slowly exhale. Relax and feel peace...

Everything feels soft and comfortable like you are being wrapped up in a soft, warm blanket. As you relax more, you feel much more at ease. If you could go deeper, you feel much better. If you could feel better, you go much deeper. That's right...

You are beginning to feel the truth. And the truth is you have now become one with the abundant universe. The universe is a deep source of supply. Visualize prosperity. You are a success story. You open yourself up, welcome and receive abundance. You are able to recognize opportunities. You seize opportunities. You are able to create wealth. You attract prosperity and abundance. They flow freely in your life. You now clearly understand the law of the universe. You receive what you attract. So when you focus on abundance and prosperity, you attract success. When you give freely, you also receive freely. You allow yourself to take the path of success. You will always have plenty. You are focused on your goals. You see them through completion. You can achieve anything with this conviction.

Repeat these words after me. Say it with your mind... "Positive attracts positive..." Think and act like someone who has plenty. And positive opportunities that you deserve flow freely. You are ready for success. You feel secure emotionally, physically and financially...

Say it again, "Positive attracts positive." You are able. You are capable. You are positive. You have plenty. From this moment on, you walk with proudly. You hold your head high because you are successful. You reflect success and abundance through your actions. You radiate positivity and prosperity. "Positive attracts positive..."

That's it... Now on the count of three, you can drift back to the present. Slowly open your eyes. You feel nicer, calmer and more positive. Open your eyes with a smile. Allow the positive energy to come out from within you. One... Two... Three...

To Accomplish your Goals

You want success in your life. You desire abundance and prosperity. You attract positivity. You have decided to move forward and beyond any blockages, blockages to success. You are committed to your goals. You focus on accomplishment. You allow yourself to experience reward, satisfaction and sense of accomplishment. You now realize that you have the capacity and amazing skills to achieve your goals. You are dedicated and persistent. You persevere in your endeavours. You are successful...

To Become Assertive

You are a smart and capable person. You contribute something meaningful. You have excellent ideas. The people around you appreciate your ideas because they are excellent and cutting edge. You are original. You believe in yourself and your ability to generate great ideas. You stand by your excellent ideas. You speak up. You stand and demonstrate your knowledge. People respect you for your courage.

You give a hundred percent in everything that you do. You enjoy making positive contributions to the team. You welcome every opportunity to demonstrate your abilities. You realize that you become better, smarter and more capable as you give more. You understand the importance of performing at your best. You always go the extra mile. You always make sure to share your ideas to others. Sharing ideas make you feel excited. You enjoy volunteering your abilities. You know that you can make a positive difference when you are proactive.

You are a natural leader. People respect and follow you. You feel proud about yourself, your ideas and your abilities to produce. Because of your enthusiasm, your love for sharing, you always succeed...

Chapter 20

Reminders about Hypnosis

Now that you know about the various problems that hypnosis can cure, it's also important to keep in mind things that can help you become successful with hypnosis, too.

What are these things? Read on and find out!

1. **Don't be too hard on yourself.** Hypnosis is supposed to make you feel relaxed, and of course, while you're under it, it's easy to actually just let go of the ill feelings and relax. However, if you feel like you're stumbling your way through, and that you're reverting to your old habits, don't be too hard on yourself.

Remember that just like anything else in life, you need a lot of practice in order to be good at this. That has actually been reiterated in a number of chapters in this book. You cannot expect yourself to be an expert in hypnosis just like that.

Think of yourself as a child who's only learning how to talk or walk. Does the child stop trying? No, he doesn't. Even if the words he speaks are incoherent at first, he still keeps on trying, and eventually, he learns how to speak. He may stumble at first, but sooner or later, he learns how to walk—even run! In short, you would only adapt the new behavior completely if you do not give up!

2. **Listen and Listen More.** Hypnosis involves the use of reinforcement tapes that would tell you the mantra that you have to invoke, or whatever it is that you have to retrieve from your mind. Make sure that you listen to it every day for a week, and every other day for the subsequent weeks. This way, you get to help yourself adapt to hypnosis, and it would make it easier for you to relax and tap into the deepest parts of your brain during the next session.

It's also extremely therapeutic because you get to quiet your brain, and opens your subconscious mind. It helps you visualize, and helps you gain more focus. Empower yourself with the tapes and you will surely learn how to go through the whole process of hypnosis well.

Take it a day at a time, though. Remember that this is not survival of the fittest, and it's definitely not a race either. You don't have to listen to all the tapes in a day alone—that would be too taxing, and would make hypnosis lose its meaning! Work at your own pace.

3. **Work on the issues that you want gone.** While you're in trance, try to work on the issues in your life that you want to change, or be eliminated. It does not matter if they're big or small. What matters is that once you tap into that mem-

ory, you begin to tell yourself that you have to work on this, and that things have to change, or else, you probably would not feel good about yourself, and your efforts would not be worth it.

Since your subconscious works in various ways, it's important that recognize a good sign when you see it. This means that you do have to understand that the memories you're able to trigger are those that you have to work on. They're the things that would make life more worthwhile for you, and that's why you have to focus on them. Don't dismiss them because it would mean that you went through hypnosis for nothing.

When positive things begin to happen, especially on your command, that's when you'd see the beauty of hypnosis—so work on those issues early on!

4. **Make use of your imagination.** The great thing about imagination is that it allows you to enter different worlds. In those different worlds in your head, you tend to know yourself better, and understand that you can move past the bad things in your life.

Remember in the chapter about Synesthesia, you were told that you become more creative when you're under synthesis, right? Well, hypnosis taps that part of your brain—use it well. Again, you should not let your imagination take you nowhere. Create new scenarios in your head. Tell yourself you can be the person you want to be and you are one step closer to being there.

5. **Be attuned to what your subconscious mind tells you.** You'd get reminders from yourself once you are in the state of hypnosis. Make sure that you use those reminders to change your life once you get back to consciousness.

For example, your subconscious might tell you that you are an amazing painter; that you can tap into the deepest parts of your brain to produce some of the best artwork possible.

Well, you may feel like you are not an artist but your subconscious won't tell you this for no reason, you know? It means deep down, you are actually an artist. You have the talent. You only need the drive and the motivation—and you could bring yourself to success if you'd believe in yourself like that.

6. **Don't stop once you feel you've succeeded.** Hypnosis isn't just a one-time thing, you see. It's something you could do even if you have succeeded at first. Actually, most of the people who've gone through hypnosis have said that they did it again another time because they have seen how great it is, and how it has changed their lives for the better.

Remember, you have to be consistent. When you make hypnosis a part of your life, you experience the best changes—and that's what matters!

Conclusion

Thank you again for purchasing this book!

I hope this book was able to help you to gain a better understanding of hypnosis and to develop basic skills in using the different hypnotism techniques.

The next step is to practice what you have learned and to help other people and yourself to live a happier, healthier, and more successful life through the power of suggestion.

Finally, if you enjoyed this book, please take the time to share your thoughts and post a review on Amazon. It'd be greatly appreciated!

Thank you and good luck!

Made in the USA
Las Vegas, NV
17 May 2021

23233870R00089